THE TRANSFORMING PRESENCE

RELEASING GOD'S ABILITY WITHIN YOU

Tom McCann

GOD'S TRANSFORMING PRESENCE
Copyright © 2021 Tom McCann

Paperback ISBN: 978-1-915223-00-5

Main translation in use: AV - KJV

Scripture quotations from The Authorized (King James) Version. Rights in the Authorized Version in the United Kingdom are vested in the Crown. Reproduced by permission of the Crown's patentee, Cambridge University Press.

Scripture taken from The Passion Translation® (TPT). Copyright © 2017, 2018 by Passion & Fire Ministries, Inc. Used by permission. All rights reserved. ThePassionTranslation.com.

Scripture taken from the Holy Bible, New International Version®, NIV®. Copyright © 1973, 1978, 1984, 2011 by Biblica, Inc. ® Used by permission of Zondervan. All rights reserved worldwide.

Scripture quotations taken from the Amplified® Bible (AMPC), Copyright © 1954, 1958, 1962, 1964, 1965, 1987 by The Lockman Foundation Used by permission. www.lockman.org

Scripture quotations taken from the Amplified® Bible (AMP), Copyright © 2015 by The Lockman Foundation. Used by permission. www.lockman.org

The ESV® Bible (The Holy Bible, English Standard Version®). ESV® Text Edition: 2016. Copyright © 2001 by Crossway, a publishing ministry of Good News Publishers. The

Publisher's statement: Throughout this book the love for our God is such that whenever we refer to Him we honour with capitals. On the other hand, when referring to the devil, we refuse to acknowledge him with any honour to the point of violating grammatical rule and withholding capitalisation.

Published by
Maurice Wylie Media
Your Inspirational Christian Publisher

For more information visit
www.MauriceWylieMedia.com

Contents

Dedication

I dedicate this book to my precious family who have given me and my wife Hazel so much joy, to my son Richard, his wife Lucy, my daughter Kathy and her husband Aaron, my son Andrew, his wife Abbie and my son Steven. Also to my dearest grandchildren Ezra, Ty, Evelyn, Milo, Xander, Arthur, Libby, Otis and Bo (Boaz). My hope and prayer for you all is that you enjoy a wonderful, blessed fulfilling life abiding in the deep, intimate reality of union with the indwelling Christ.

Acknowledgements

I had never considered writing a book. However, after retiring from business in 2015 the Lord gave me a strong desire to start putting on paper some of the key truths He had taught me. Although I wasn't sure if it would ever go to print I hoped that maybe in some small way, if I could share it with others, He would use it to help those who struggled with the same issues as I had.

From my earliest days my parents impressed on me the vital importance of spiritual realities. Their lives left an indelible imprint on my heart to the point that I could never just drift with the crowd. I had to find and know the God they knew and experience Him in the cut and thrust of every day life just as they had.

I am deeply indebted to Gunner Olsen, the anointed founder of ICCC, the visionary Michael Fenton-Jones and the teaching of Peter Michell. These men expanded my vision of what God could do in my life and encouraged me never to settle for less than all God had for me.

Other significant influences came from authors whose books brought incredibly light and clarity to my heart. Several from the pen of Andrew Murray. Beverly Carradine's book "The Sanctified Life" and "The Victorious Life" by an unknown author were major landmarks. I also delved into the writings from some of the old mystics, in particular Madame Guyon and Father Fenelon even though I struggled with some of what they had to say. However, after the Bible, the greatest benefit by far came from the writings of Norman Grubb and his teaching on union with Christ.

I am indebted to my very good friend Stephen Gunning for working his way through a very long, unedited first draft and for his encouragement, input and suggestions. Also to Wilf Carter and David Calvert for their valued feed back after reading the manuscript and their ongoing support and encouragement. Thank you also to Brian Graham and Sam McKilrath for reading extracts from later versions and providing some very helpful insights, both from a doctrinal perspective as well as textually.

There is however one person to whom I owe more that I can possibly say, my loving, patient supportive, selfless wife, Hazel. She has been my constant companion on life's journey and God's incredible gift to me. This book you hold in your hands would simply never have got past the first draft but for her tireless willingness to read and re-read the multiple drafts and helping me to say in a few words what I would normally say in ten. Thank you Hazel for your love, encouragement and patience.

Finally, none of this would ever have happened but for the incredible mercy and kindness of the One who so graciously came into my life and turned my world right side up, the Lord Jesus Himself, the Teacher of all teachers, my All in All! All credit and honour for whatever is of benefit to those who read these pages goes to Him alone!

Introduction

It's clear from Scripture that there is a place in God where He becomes real to us, the cornerstone of our lives, and this internal well-spring of supernatural life gushes out from our inner man. It is nothing less than the indwelling reality of the living Christ in all His competence and power, revealing Himself as our rescuer, our high tower, the source of our transformation and our all-inclusive supply!

As a young Christian however, I often felt something was missing, not only in my own life but also in the Christian community to which I belonged. I wasn't sure what it was but I felt that I and many sincere, devout Christians were struggling. It was obvious there was a lack of the overflow and joy promised in the Bible. I could see a lot of dedication and earnestness. I could identify a great deal of effort being expended in trying to serve the Lord and to be pleasing to Him. However I couldn't see much evidence of this abundant life which Jesus had promised.

I could never see the point of maintaining christian traditions for their own sake. Branches don't grow on trees because that is how it has always been in the past, but because the life in them works itself out in that way! That is the divine order! This makes the central issue one of LIFE, not form or any other external appendage. As a result I struggled to fit into the accepted forms and external expressions of what christianity looked like. I felt much of it was the external leftovers from a reality enjoyed by bygone generations but which had now lost its core vibrancy and vitality. To me it felt like the dying embers of a fire that once burnt brightly! This bothered me deeply and it birthed a profound longing to find what I thought was missing. Instinctively I knew the answer would not be found in a watered down, superficial, populist version of Christianity which asks little and delivers even less. I wanted the real thing so to speak and not be just vaccinated with it.

All we can do is to start our search from the position in which we find ourselves and with the understanding we have at that time. In my case that resulted in much of my effort and time being wasted following false trails and going down rabbit holes which led nowhere. I had to unlearn much of what I had learnt. My search was very much characterised by discovering what didn't work before I could find what did work. When your back is against the wall it is quite amazing how quickly it focuses the mind and bends the knee! How quickly pressure can remove the tinsel and dross from our lives, forcing us to go deeper than we would otherwise have gone. I have recognised, that in my life, pressure has often been God's calling card as He sought to get my attention so He could lead me into a deeper revelation of Himself as the amazing deliverer and rescuer that He is!

Much of the emphasis in contemporary Christianity is predicated on the need to educate the intellect. It analyses biblical text, historic context, and so on, seeking to draw out every nuance of truth to enhance our understanding. Biblical knowledge, however, is not the key that delivers "abundant life." A correct understanding of biblical truth is vital, but on its own, it leaves us still operating one step removed from the one true source of "life." The reality is, *"The natural man receiveth not the things of the Spirit of God ... **because they are spiritually discerned"*** (1 Corinthians 2:14). We must never allow our search for biblical knowledge and a deeper understanding of Scripture to outstrip our focus on what is the primary central issue, which is the personal reality of Jesus Himself "who is our life"!

Christianity does not function at the level of our intellect; it functions in a totally different realm. Biblical Christianity is "Spirit" sourced. This immediately takes us into a very different realm of "knowing"!

It was many years before I was able to identify what was missing and that for which I had been searching. I discovered the answer to all my searching was the deep, intimate reality of union with Christ! This opens us up to the enjoyment of the indwelling presence of Christ in a way we could never anticipate or imagine!

This search for fulfilment, contentment, and satisfaction is one of humanity's deepest longings and highest motivators. However, discovering it in the melé of voices within Christendom is not as easy as one might think. Having found it, I can say it is well worth the search, for it exceeds our wildest expectations and takes us into realms of contentment and satisfaction beyond anything we could ever have imagined.

In the following chapters I will share, not just some of my own experience, but I will expose the very root of why many of us struggle with a sense of alienation and separation from His Presence. We will uncover the full force of His ability to rescue and deliver us from all our enemies, inside and out! My desire is to chart the route to the centre, to the very sanctuary of His Presence dwelling within. This is where life can be lived in effortless intimacy, in the spontaneous overflow of the new creation identity in Christ.

Tom McCann

Chapter 1

How to Get Out of a Tight Spot

It was another Monday morning! As I made my way into the office, the long queue of traffic moved slowly along the West Link in Belfast, Northern Ireland, but my mind was racing, going over all I needed to do when I got there. My thoughts were interrupted by a call from one of our Service Engineers. He had been scheduled to visit a customer who had recently bought a large machine from us but which had developed teething problems. Upon arriving, he had been denied entry and, to make matters worse, the owner of the company, who had just left for a three-month holiday in Florida, had left instructions demanding the machine be removed from his factory.

At just over £360k this had been a reasonably good order for us. It was physically a very large machine, 15 or 16 meters in length and 5 or 6 meters high, weighing over 40 tons. It took the best part of a month simply to erect it on site. Most customers naturally want their "pound of flesh" and drive a hard bargain; however, this one made others look like amateurs. They were exacting and very hard to please. Nevertheless, we always seemed to get along despite regular "head-to-head" confrontations.

At this particular time, I, along with my fellow directors, was not welcome on site due to one of these disagreements, and the owner had refused to take my calls. Our sales manager and our service engineers were the only ones with whom he would speak.

Upon completing this installation, we had undertaken an acceptance test which had gone well. We received a small deposit with the order but before any further funds were to be paid, they wanted to run the machine for a few weeks. It was here that we ran into difficulties. Although there was a run of small faults which occurred intermittently, we were able to fix them. However, other more serious faults began to occur and after several weeks of very poor reliability, relations became very tense indeed.

The customer had now clearly lost confidence in the machine and in our ability to eliminate the down-time he was experiencing. This was potentially catastrophic! Besides the financial implications which, in themselves, were extremely serious, logistically it raised insurmountable difficulties for us. It would take weeks to dismantle and, when it was dismantled, how could we store it as we had no facilities large enough? Also, even when we had ironed out all the faults, how could we sell it to another customer if news of its unreliability got into the marketplace? Our competitors would have a field day!

When I got into the office I immediately rang the Number Two in charge at the company, but he was adamant that our engineers were not going to be allowed on site to attempt further repairs and insisted that the machine needed to be removed. There was nothing I could say or do to persuade him differently; he was not going to countermand the owner's instructions. After a lengthy and very difficult call I put the phone down. As I leaned back into my chair I had two very different responses going on inside me at the same time. All the potential implications of this situation began to tumble into my mind, and I realised that we were in very serious trouble. I could see no way out and could think of nothing that would prevent this from badly hurting the company. On another level, I still had my peace, and I knew that Jesus was Lord of my life, even this life I was living this Monday morning, facing, what for me, was an impossible situation. I remember very clearly thinking that, at one level, this crisis was not so much my problem as it was His.

I can understand that may seem a very strange reaction to some. To the natural mind I was now very much in the "hot seat." However, I had learnt not to simply see my situation through the natural lens alone. I was aware of Christ's presence with me, so I instinctively knew to allow Him to carry this challenge. "The government was on His shoulders" not mine, and He would be much better at dealing with this than I would. The unchanging reality for all of us who are born of the Spirit is that *"...greater is He that is in you,* (whatever the crisis may be) *than he that is in the world"* (1 John 4:4, parentheses mine)

I decided, since there was nothing practical I could do, that I would go up to a nearby park for a coffee. I needed to go somewhere where I could be alone and talk to the Lord and get His take on what was happening. Since, in one way, I didn't feel this problem was up to me to solve, I simply asked the Lord what He was going to do about it and how did He want me to respond? I read a few Scriptures and then waited in silence for Him to make clear what I should do next.

As I waited, I began to feel that I should actually ring the owner in Florida. However, to my natural mind that didn't make any sense at all. I was *persona non grata,* and the last person he would want to hear from. Indeed, he had put the phone down on me the last time we spoke and had refused to take any more of my calls. If he refused my calls when he was at work, why would he accept one now? Surely he would be even more belligerent and difficult to deal with if I had the nerve to intrude on his holiday. More to the point, in the unlikely event he accepted my call, what could I say to him? It would be a very difficult conversation. I asked the Lord for favour and felt I should simply "speak to the mountain" and decree favour and good will, binding all hostility and anger from coming against me. I also felt the Lord gave me a practical proposal to submit to the owner in order to assure him that we could actually resolve these ongoing problems.

I drove back to the office and because of the different time zones waited until after lunch to ring the customer. I asked if he was free to speak and quickly became aware that he was behaving differently towards me compared to how he normally conducted himself. He was friendly and polite, extremely obliging and, without any hesitation, agreed to accept my proposal in full. I was completely taken aback with this change. Indeed, I don't think we ever had such a civil conversation in all the twenty or more years I had known this man. As the conversation came to an end what he said totally blew me away. It was something along these lines. "Tom, I don't understand why I am being so nice to you nor why I am agreeing to go along with your proposal. I'm not normally like this."

This was the key that unlocked the entire situation. Over the following weeks I was able to implement the proposal I felt the Lord had given me, and the customer was soon satisfied with the machine. It has since proven itself to be a great asset, enhancing the company's capability and competitiveness.

Of course, in my early days as a Christian, I had not always seen God as someone I could go to for help in the everyday challenges I faced. Neither did I know His presence as an ongoing inner reality. Yes, He had forgiven me, and that was such a release from the burden and fear I had felt about meeting Him one day, but I still saw Him as a faraway deity. I felt that He had such high expectations, and I had my work cut out for me if I was ever going to be able to please Him.

You see, I was operating from a mindset that it was all up to me to make it in life and to live in a way that would be acceptable to Him. I had only one outlook and that was what I could grasp with my natural mind and my physical senses in the everyday circumstances of my life. The spiritual realm was a faraway land that I had only heard about, but I had no awareness of it and as I said, neither had I any sense of the nearness and intimacy of the Lord's presence. Back then it felt like He was separated and disconnected from the life I was living. I'm so grateful that God didn't leave me there. I want to share in the following pages the story of how this all changed.

Chapter 2

If I Have It All, Where Is It?

I was born in Brazil where my parents were missionaries. I left them in my mid-teens and traveled back alone to Northern Ireland where I lived in a home for young adults whose parents were on the mission field. As a young teenager newly arrived in a different country this was a real shock to the system. I struggled to settle into an unfamiliar culture and work ethic. The language, the dark clouds, and endless rainy weather, the strait-laced culture, the fact that the "Troubles"[1] were just kicking off all combined to shock me into a new reality for which I was not prepared.

Like most Christians, I believed what the Bible said about Christ coming into us when we got saved, but as I said, I had very little awareness of that fact. My experience was still one of, "I'm down here and He is away up there somewhere." It seemed to me that most Christians I knew had a similar outlook. Their conversation and the way they prayed were all from the perspective of a God who was outside of them, seated far away in Heaven.

The conservative evangelical circle in which I grew up placed a very strong emphasis on acquiring biblical knowledge. The study of the Scriptures was seen as the key route to an overcoming and victorious

---

1 "Troubles" was an ethno-nationalist conflict in Northern Ireland which came to the fore in the late 1960s continuing until the signing of the Good Friday Agreement on the 10th of April 1998. In total over 3,000 people lost their lives.

life. It also had a strong external emphasis. It was a culture that majored on appearance and form. There was an acceptable "look" for both men and women which was mostly a throwback to styles of the forties and fifties. There was also a list of so-called "spiritual" activities which needed to be followed. Attendance at all meetings was expected. In public prayer the use of old English pronouns, such as "thee" and "thou," was mandatory. It was a language all its own, and the preaching was no different. It was delivered in a completely unnatural tone of voice. I could never get my head around that one. Watching TV or playing sports were serious misdemeanours. God had forgiven me but now I found myself having to comply with this rigid, artificial, external code of appearance and conduct.

My default outlook, however, was on an external God who sat back and watched what I did and how I managed myself. Although I knew I was saved I also had a strong feeling that He would be very quick to crack me on the knuckles if I stepped out of line. I had very little awareness of God's love for me beyond a mere mental knowledge that He did love me. My awareness of God was more that of a judge who scrutinised every detail of my life, taking note of every little failure and lapse. To me at that time He was a hard, maybe even a harsh, demanding, all-powerful being who made impossible demands of me.

After I arrived in Northern Ireland, one of the first big decisions I faced was what I was going to do now. I was completely unprepared to make this decision at every level. I had no idea how I could know God's will for my life or what He wanted me to do. It was no different on the practical level of knowing what jobs were out there and where I would fit in. I was stuck and struggling to find my way. I had been advised to serve my time in a local aircraft manufacturing company but hated every minute I was there. The grim reality of where I found myself made me grow up quickly indeed. However, I knew I had to get on with it and knuckle down, hoping that God would have mercy on me. Nevertheless, I was unsettled and restless.

One night, on a break during night shift, I went out to my car in the parking lot. It had a soft top so I put the roof down to enjoy the clear sky and full moon of the beautiful crisp winter's night. As I sat there in the stillness, my thoughts turned to what I had left behind in Brazil just a little over three years before and compared it to the situation in which I now found myself. My frustration and restlessness welled up in an involuntary, agonising cry to God. I looked up to heaven, raised both my arms, and cried out in distress, "Lord! Surely you must have something more for me than this! Is this all you have for me? Please show me what you want me to do with my life!"

To my great astonishment I was immediately conscious that God had heard me and, inwardly, I clearly felt Him say to me, "Go home, buy the Belfast Telegraph which has all the jobs advertised and apply for any positions you think would suit you. Once you've done that leave the rest to me, do nothing else." This felt like my thoughts had taken on a life of their own. I knew they didn't originate with me. I was surprised by this as I had no expectation that God would respond so immediately and directly to my prayer. This was a very real, personal, and intimate form of communication. It hinted that there was another side to this remote, all-powerful God beyond what I had realised, but the full significance didn't quite hit me at the time.

I sent away four letters applying for four different positions which sounded interesting. After several interviews over a period of nine months with one of those companies, I took up my new position. I had been tempted many times to apply for other posts because of the nine-month delay but I am so glad I didn't. I worked for this company for the next forty-one years and over time was promoted through the ranks and ended up running the company. I retired at the end of 2015.

The company sold machine tools and serviced the machines they supplied. These were the same sorts of machines I had learnt to use when I worked in the aircraft company. All that mind-numbing time which I thought was wasted was, in fact, preparation for the next step God had in store for me.

As I took on added responsibility at work, I became more earnest in my desire to honour God with my life. I had been taught that there was no "second blessing" or subsequent experience of a deeper filling of the Holy Spirit beyond "getting saved." I had been taught that once saved you got everything you needed in the one package and it was really up to me, albeit with God's help of course, to then put it all to work as best I could. Yes, Jesus had died for me and had saved me; however, it was now up to me to "work out my own salvation" by my own willpower, discipline, and ability. Since I had been taught I already "had it all" I felt that I must surely already have the resources that I needed to live as He would want me to live.

That was all well and good. However, as time passed, I found it wasn't that easy. I struggled to live up to the required standard I thought God expected, so naturally I did the only thing I could do which was to redouble my efforts by putting into practice all the usual Christian disciplines I was taught. I tried to pray and read my Bible more. I tried to be more holy and more committed while sticking to all the rules. I thought this would surely empower me to live in a way which would be pleasing to God.

As young Christians we were taught to study the Scriptures. However, I had never been much of a student. I was more of an active, outdoors sort of person rather than the passive, reflective, studious type. It was obvious to me that, if this was the way to progress spiritually, I was going to struggle. I can't tell you the number of times I tried. I started all sorts of Bible courses, used many different daily reading notes, and sought to employ different methods designed to facilitate the reluctant student. I always gave up, however, and was never able to be consistent. It always seemed so dry, and I struggled to understand the context and practical application of what I read.

Although it is glaringly obvious to me now, it wasn't then. There is a world of difference between seeking biblical knowledge and seeking the author Himself in an up-close and intimate way.

Why did I find reading the Bible so difficult? If I already had everything, where was it and why did it feel like it wasn't operational and working as I thought it should in my life? Why was I always coming up short? Where was the enjoyment and reality of this abundant life Jesus had promised? And why was most of my prayer time spent in trying unsuccessfully to extricate myself from under a dark blanket of condemnation and guilt for continually missing the mark as I saw it? It's not surprising then that when it came to sharing my faith, although I felt a duty to do it, it felt feeble and artificial.

As a result, I started asking much deeper questions of myself. It was becoming obvious to me that the person I was having the most difficulty with was me. I was my own biggest problem! Although I knew I was saved, my experience was one of weakness and lack rather than victory. This was not what I had expected! I had been taught that the by-product of becoming a Christian was victory over the habits that defeated me, over impure thoughts, over fears, and over the areas where my conduct did not match what I knew God expected. I found that I was still very self-centred, impatient, and inconsiderate. My love for God was often cold and there was not much left over for others either. In truth God seemed to be far away and separate from the life I was living.

I remember in my early twenties I had the opportunity, after a meeting, to talk with the preacher about how I was feeling. I wanted help so I could overcome in my thought life, particularly in the area of purity. His reply stunned me. When I asked him how I could overcome he said, "What are you? A man or a mouse?" Well, that brought an abrupt end to that conversation. I went away feeling about two inches tall! That wasn't the only thing that surprised me though. What really took me to the fair was the fact that, in his opinion, victory was gained by will power. I was shocked that this preacher wasn't able to show me how I could overcome temptation and sin. That to me, even then, was such an elementary question, yet here he was, a highly respected and much sought-after preacher telling me the answer was to try harder. I felt pretty certain he was wrong on that point but I couldn't have said in what way. I was no different than every other young Christian man who wanted to be pure and overcome, so why had he no solution to offer me?

I quickly concluded that if all Christianity could offer me was my own will power, then I was no better equipped to handle life's challenges than someone who had never heard about Christ. Besides, I was certain from what I saw expressed in many Scriptures that they promised a power, an inner adequacy that would deliver victory if only I could get to grips with how it worked. For now, however, it seemed to be outside of my experience.

The preachers I heard week in and week out were all very good at exhorting us to "live for Jesus," to be pure, holy, more loving and patient, to stick to the rules, to be bold evangelists, and on and on the list went. They very eloquently presented the case for each of these essential traits. However, I don't think I ever heard anyone explain how I could tap into the power that would actually enable me to do all these things. My understanding was that becoming a Christian would naturally make me a better person, yet that was clearly not happening—for me anyway!

To compound my predicament, I saw many Scriptures which talked about other inner realities that were also mostly outside my experience. Take, for example, *"so that Christ may dwell in your hearts through faith, ... may have power, ... to grasp how wide and long and high and deep is the love of Christ, and to know this love that surpasses knowledge—that you may be filled to the measure of all the fullness of God"* (Ephesians 3:17-19 NIV). I was somewhat confused by the fact that Paul prayed this prayer for Christians because did they not already know that Christ was in them? Also, did they not already know God loved them? Of course, intellectually I also knew Christ had taken up residence within and that God loved me but I had never "felt" that He loved me, nor had I any consciousness of Christ as an indwelling reality. It's clear to me today that Paul wanted more for them than simply having that information. He was praying for something they could experience, something which "surpassed knowledge." Also, the last portion of the verse promises the possibility of something so immense and so far removed from what I then thought was possible—the possibility that I could be *filled to the measure of all the fullness of God*! The Amplified Classic puts it this way, "... *that you may be filled through all your being unto all the fullness of God, that you may have the richest measure of the divine Presence, and become a body, wholly filled and flooded with God Himself!*"

This was tantalising to me but also profoundly unsettling! If I already had everything as I had been taught, how come this was not a reality to me? More to the point, why would Paul pray that they "may have the richest measure of the divine Presence, and become a body, wholly filled and flooded with God Himself" if those Christians already had it all?

Back then this promise captivated my thinking and created a deep unrest and dissatisfaction with my Christian walk. I was forced to embark on a search for more not knowing where it would end!

Chapter 3

What to Do When It's Not Working

When I met the lovely girl who was to become my wife we often talked about the Lord, and it soon became clear to me that her relationship with Him was very different to mine. From the first time we went out together one of the things that most attracted me to Hazel, beyond her good looks, was her genuine and unassuming honesty and transparency. She had a great sense of humour and a level of integrity I had seldom witnessed before. Intriguingly, there was also a freedom in her walk with the Lord, and she didn't seem to have all the hang ups I was experiencing in my relationship with Him. We got married in 1977.

On one level life was very good—mainly due to Hazel's positive influence. I had left behind most of my angst about leaving Brazil and no longer hankered after the life I enjoyed there. I was happy to be in Northern Ireland despite the "Troubles" as I knew this was where God had placed me and He had the bigger picture in hand. However, on another level I was dissatisfied with my experience as a Christian. The more I got into the Scriptures the more unsettled I became. I was hungry because, by now, I was fairly convinced there actually was a great deal more to be experienced beyond receiving forgiveness and the assurance of Heaven at the end of the road. However, what that "more" looked like or how I could come into the enjoyment of it was a mystery to me.

I also regularly talked to other mature Christians within our community, people we highly respected and trusted. At one level they were quite willing to acknowledge things were not in great shape and were willing to accept that there was a clear disparity between what Scripture promised and their own experience. The usual explanation given, as an attempt to legitimise this disparity, was expressed by saying, "Positionally we are correct but conditionally we fall short." This seemed to entirely miss the point and, for me, it was ludicrous to settle for a mere theoretical "positional correctness"[2] that lacked the corresponding inner reality or substance outworked in my life.

There seemed to be a very real resistance to even acknowledge that a change in emphasis might be needed, as to do so seemed to challenge the "intellectual correctness" of the biblical knowledge which was so highly prized. I was beginning to realise that, despite this biblical emphasis, we can't live the Christian life out of doctrine any more than we can fly because we understand the laws of aerodynamics. I realised that I had fallen into the trap of thinking that a mental knowledge of truth was the same thing as it actually being operational in my life. This is a very subtle mindset. Biblical knowledge is cerebral but experiencing the vital, dynamic reality to which it points requires a significant work of the Spirit in our hearts—something entirely different!

I understood that Jesus came to set the captives free but I knew that freedom didn't consist of a continual battle within myself, trying to keep myself on the straight and narrow by suppressing what was inside. Freedom, by definition, must mean the struggle is over and the battle has been won. Neither could freedom be living under compulsion or law or even dutiful strained obedience. Instinctively I knew that true freedom, from a Scriptural perspective, meant being myself, living spontaneously from my heart yet knowing that, in doing so, I was

2 Positional correctness - This expression was used to refer to a theological "correctness" that informed how church government and church order was practised. This then allowed the membership to have an understanding that they were "correct" in God's eyes even though in their everyday lives things may not all have been as they should.

pleasing my Father. As the early church father, St. Augustine of Hippo, is reputed to have said in the third century, "Love God and do whatever you please."[3] Hadn't Jesus promised, *"If the Son therefore shall make you free, ye shall be free indeed?"* (John 8:36).

I could probably have learnt to accept the way things were back then if I had been able to find the answers to the deeper questions I was asking. However, it was becoming clear to me that something was missing. I was sure of one thing though: The question as to how I could find the power to live this victorious, abundant life would not be answered by my compliance to a man-made straight jacket or, for that matter, to any externally imposed code of conduct.

Indeed, I began to feel there was something wrong with me and that my experience of God was defective. I felt alone in feeling this way since most of those around me seemed quite happy with the way things were. However, I see now that I was keeping very good company indeed. Paul vented similar frustration… *"For I do not understand my own actions. I do not practice or accomplish what I wish, but I do the very thing that I loathe. … I can will what is right, but I cannot perform it. For I fail to practice the good deeds I desire to do, but the evil deeds that I do not desire to do are what I am doing"* (Romans 7:15-19 AMPC).

I found myself at a fork in the road. Either I could face up to the reality of my failure and weakness and press in to find my sufficiency in Christ or I could keep my mask firmly in place and carry on just as I was. Maintaining the "status quo," however, was never really an option.

I was yet to discover that the Christian life is not lived by striving and self-effort, by struggling to keep external rules and so-called "Christian" norms. I was still labouring under the illusion that I needed to try harder, be more committed, pray more, read my Bible more, and serve Jesus more, all in the hope that, at some point, I would find this

---

3 Augustine of Hippo, from *"Homilies on the First Epistle of John."*

abundant life. I was still to learn the critical lesson Paul learnt when He said, *"For I know that nothing good lives in me, that is, in my flesh"* (Romans 7:18 AMPC). Paul was real and up front. He didn't seek to put a positive spin on his poor performance, nor did he find comfort in his "correct doctrine" or "positional correctness" glossing over his unhappy experience. He cried out in utter despair of himself, *"O unhappy and pitiable and wretched man that I am! Who will release and deliver me from the shackles of this body of death?"* (Romans 7:15-24 AMPC).

We moved to a small village outside Lisburn and heard about a group of Christians who were meeting together in a house some 10 miles away. We decided to visit them and found they were around the same age and from a similar doctrinal background. It was refreshing to hear that they were asking the same questions we were.

Several months later, after a lot of heart searching and prayer, we decided to leave our assembly and join this small house group. This was a massive step for us as it meant leaving our familiar and comfortable confines behind. It was opening the door to the unknown and to the possibility of getting it all very wrong indeed. It meant leaving all those we deeply respected and loved. We are so grateful to the Lord for the Godly deposit left in us during those early years but now we felt we were being squeezed and constricted by external norms which held no water. The old wine skins had lost their wine, at least for us. This caused a lot of hurt to our loved ones and extended family circle. That was not what we wanted at all, and we would have done anything to avoid it. Nevertheless, the choice for me was clear: We could continue living as we were or we could follow God's leading in the hope that He would bring us into that for which we were searching. Other peoples' feelings, no matter how much we respected and loved them, could not place a veto on something so vital and elemental as this.

We enjoyed a freedom in our small group that we had not experienced before. There was an informality and honesty which was very refreshing.

The masks came off and we became more transparent with our close fellow believers. We couldn't wait for Sunday to come around so we could meet again and talk about the Lord and worship Him together.

It felt so strange to feel this way. We were enjoying this far too much! No matter what else was going on we never wanted to miss getting together. This was in marked contrast to how we had felt when we went to meetings out of duty. There was an excitement and a joy as we pressed into God.

During our Bible studies we found ourselves, time and again, asking questions about the Holy Spirit. How could we square the circle between what we believed i.e., that we "got it all" when we got saved as we had been taught, and our meagre experience, the obvious lack of power, and the shallow inner witness of the Spirit's presence? At that time I didn't think it was even possible to know the awareness of the abiding, indwelling presence of Christ.

As a group we started asking questions around spiritual gifts. What about prophecy, tongues, words of knowledge, gifts of healing, etc.? We began to seriously question the theological position we had learnt, that these gifts had all passed away and were no longer for today. This was an exciting time! It was a time of real hunger and searching where we had to consider possibilities we had previously discounted.

It was the following year that we as a family headed off for a break. Hazel, myself, our two children and our house group attended a conference in Prestatyn in Wales, called Spring Harvest '83. There were seminars on various subjects during the day and meetings in the "Big Top" tent each morning and evening.

We arrived and got settled into the little chalets which were to be our accommodations for the week. A babysitting service was available which allowed parents to go to the evening meetings. Excitement was high as this was a totally new experience for all of us and we felt we were on the cusp of something new.

Graham Kendrick was leading the worship for the week, and there were a number of well-known speakers to take the morning and evening sessions. That first night Floyd McClung, European Director of YWAM, spoke. He came across with such authority, authenticity, and conviction. It was clear that he knew experientially what he was talking about. This was to be no superficial message where he regurgitated ideas or theoretical spiritual concepts picked up from books. He was speaking about walking by faith in everyday life and how essential this was in order to please God.

I listened with utmost attention, drinking in every word. I had never heard anything like this before. Then he made a statement that I will never forget. It shook me to my very core. He said, "*We have not begun to live the life of faith until we are living beyond the realm of our own ability.*" I was stunned by this! This was immense and carried wide implications for my life! It opened up to me the possibility of a life where my feeble ability and performance would no longer be the determining factor. This fired a deep yearning within me, and I just knew this was the reality for which I had been searching.

During the week we all went to seminars on various topics of interest. Paul, the leader of our small group went to one on the subject of the baptism of the Spirit. He had gone in with a fixed understanding that the Spirit came into us at conversion and there was no "second blessing" to be had. He was fairly adamant on that point. However, as he listened to the message, he found himself being overcome by a consciousness of the love of God for him personally and by the immediacy of the Lord's very presence. The Lord revealed Himself to him in a very gentle and loving way. After a while he found himself saying words which did not originate from his mind. They were spontaneous utterances, what Scripture calls speaking in tongues. He was blown away by this, and it overrode all his previous resistance to spiritual gifts.

When he shared this afterwards with our group, the effect on me was electric. Here was someone who wasn't "flaky," yet God had met him in an "out of the box" way. I thought, If God could meet him in such a real way, then there was no reason why He wouldn't do the same for me.

There were no meetings planned for the afternoon so I decided to get alone with God and do some business with Him. As I unburdened myself before Him I confessed my weakness and frustration. I repented of everything I could think of and asked Him to have mercy on me and to lead me into all He had for me. My frustration and emptiness poured out as I longed to experience Him in all His fullness. I could no longer accept my feeble Christian experience as the norm.

I stayed before Him and waited. I prayed, I read a few Scriptures, I prayed again but didn't seem to be making much progress. As I continued to wait a Scripture reference popped into my head. It was Psalm 18 so I looked it up: *"The Lord is my Rock, my Fortress, and my Deliverer; my God, my keen and firm Strength in Whom I will trust and take refuge, my Shield, and the Horn of my salvation, my High Tower ... so shall I be saved from my enemies"* and so it goes on, declaring God as our Deliverer and the One who equips us and teaches us how to overcome. Yes, that is what I wanted. Lord, *"teach my hands how to do war, enable me to overtake my enemies and defeat them! Illumine my darkness! Cause me to be an overcomer, Lord,"* I prayed.

These words verbalised perfectly what I was desperately seeking, and I was grateful that God had brought this Psalm to my attention. However, I was disappointed as well as I wanted to know and experience the reality of what this Psalm was saying so I stayed on my knees, telling the Lord that I wasn't going anywhere until He gave me or promised me that for which I was looking.

As I waited, another Scripture reference popped into my mind. I quickly turned to 2 Samuel chapter 22 and to my utter amazement, I found that it was verbatim what I had found in Psalm 18. Now was that a coincidence? I didn't believe so. It was very clear that God was speaking to me directly. This was not God just giving me words that described what I was searching for, but He was making me a very specific, clear promise. God was promising me that He Himself would be my fortress, my rescuer and deliverer, and that He would teach me how I could overcome all my enemies, inside and out, just as the Psalm described. There was zero emotion, it was just a simple faith transaction. A new confidence now welled up from within. No deep emotional or spiritual experience but then I hadn't been looking for an experience, I had been looking for much, much more. I got up from my knees feeling like all my burdens and concerns had been lifted off my shoulders. A deep stillness and calm settled within. As I stood up, I knew I had encountered God and that He had His hand on me and I could trust Him to lead me into all that He had for me.

The following morning we were running late to get to the meeting in the big tent. By the time we got the children settled in crèche we could only find a seat near the back. Graham Kendrick had already started leading the worship. As I stood there and closed my eyes, I pondered the beautiful words being sung by this massive crowd. It was then that something quite unexpected happened. I began to experience a fresh release as my heart spontaneously welled up in worship and a heartfelt longing to express the utter wonder and awesome beauty of this amazing Jesus. His outrageous grace and tender patience toward me, His immense love for me and commitment to me caused my heart to break and overflow with unrestrained gratitude and deep worship. I couldn't help but raise my hands and give myself to Him in praise and adoration! This was the first time my heart spontaneously and effortlessly overflowed with such intense adoration, worship, and gratitude to the Lord. The tap had been opened and it all just poured out!

Chapter 4

Pushing the Envelope

This encounter was the start of unmasking the false god in whom I had believed. There had always been a dark undertone in how I viewed Him. Yes, I knew there was a love side to Him but there was a darker underbelly as well and, to me, this was the more dominant facet which had made me afraid. I had seen God as an uncompromising judge, demanding and hard. Love, from my perspective, was well down the list of His character traits. Now my view of Him began to alter. I was experiencing Him as a Father. His gentle love and tenderness caused me to see Him in a completely different light. For the first time I could see that He seemed to be truly good. This was where many of the misconceptions as to the nature and character of the God I had grown up with and laboured under for most of my life began to be dispelled. He didn't tolerate me, He wasn't angry or fed up with me for all my failure and sin. He still had hopes and plans for my life. He still believed in me and He wasn't done with me yet. This insight had a significant impact! I began to realise just how good God was and how much He cared and loved me personally. A lot of the fear and dread I had carried drained away. I found myself coming into a greater measure of freedom, confidence and openness in my walk with the Lord.

I had begun to believe that my problems would be resolved by receiving more of God. My Christianity had felt so weak and feeble to this point that I thought what I needed was a deeper experience of the Holy Spirit. I understood this as being "baptised in the Holy Spirit" as Acts and 1ˢᵗ Corinthians talk about, so at this time I interpreted my experience at Spring Harvest within that context. If you had asked me to explain what happened I would have said that I had received the "baptism of the Holy Spirit" although when I left the conference I had no manifestation of any of the gifts of the Spirit.

Four or five weeks later I was driving up the M2 motorway listening to a cassette tape by Derek Prince when I started to worship the Lord out loud. A few words which I didn't understand slipped in to what I was saying. They weren't English and I hadn't planned to say them but they kept coming. Words spontaneously flowed from my lips without premeditation yet completely under my control. I could start and stop at will. This was not the by-product of any ecstatic or intense spiritual experience as I was still very aware that I was driving the car on a busy motorway. It just seemed the most natural thing in the world to express my praise and gratitude to the Lord by stepping out of my logical, rational mind and moving into a Holy Spirit-enabled means of expression. That's all it was! *"For anyone who speaks in a tongue does not speak to people but to God. Indeed, no one understands them; they utter mysteries by the Spirit .... For if I pray in a tongue, my spirit prays, but my mind is unfruitful"* (1 Corinthians 14:2,14 NIV). This was how I was brought into my first experience of speaking in tongues and operating one of the gifts of the Spirit.

Something else, however, soon became clear to me. Beyond the newfound freedom and reality I had found in the Lord and in worshiping Him, I found myself becoming even more hungry for God and His Word. I began to devour it! I had found fresh water and tasted the reality of His love, and I now knew there was more to be had. I had read very few spiritual books up to that point but now I began to read books by the dozen. Every time I was in the car on business, which was almost every day, I made sure I had lots of teaching tapes with me. I was so hungry that every other interest fell away.

Whatever label is used to describe this encounter with the Lord is unimportant to me today. For me it was surely a "baptism of hunger," the like of which I had never experienced before.

I also began to feel very uncomfortable with a Christianity that was expressed only with words. I longed to experience His power and deliverance in my everyday life. First Corinthians 4:20 weighed heavily on my heart, *"For the kingdom of God is not a matter of talk but of power"* (NIV). In the original Greek it reads, *"The Kingdom of God is not in words but in power."* Despite all the meetings I had attended and all the great preachers I had listened to, I was shocked by how little "power" I had seen displayed, and I knew that would have to change.

Our little group continued to meet as His love began to dislodge some of the deep-seated misconceptions we had all carried. It opened us up to a new joy and freedom in our walk with Him and encouraged us to press in for more. Also, if this walk of faith was to mean anything it must surely be the route to finding God's supply and provision in the very real issues we faced every day.

We began to see some small breakthroughs. During one of our house meetings one of the girls shared that she had been really struggling with a sore back because one of her legs was a little shorter than the other, and this had been troubling her for a long time. Someone in our group pointed at me and asked me to pray for her. I had never prayed for healing before and felt unsure of myself. I couldn't heal her but would God respond to my prayer? I began to pray in a weak and stumbling manner and as I prayed I felt her heel, which I was holding, begin to move out and grow until both legs were the same length. We were all utterly astonished and completely taken aback with a sense of fear and awe at seeing, with our own eyes, God's greatness and power in action. It was scary seeing this happen for the first time, but we were overcome by His goodness and thanked Him for what He was doing amongst us.

On a separate occasion Hazel and I were getting ready to go to the mid-week house group. I had arrived home from work later than usual and she was trying to get our four children settled in bed. I rushed out to collect the babysitter and drove up the quiet, country road much faster than the speed limit allowed. On the way back home, I was stopped by traffic police. They had "clocked" me speeding on the way out and told me they were going to prosecute. Traffic police always followed through with prosecution and they were known for never letting anyone off so there was no way of preventing this going to court which was the norm in those days.

The incident upset me and when we came home from the meeting I went up to my room. I told the Lord I was sorry for speeding and asked if, in His mercy He could intervene as I needed my driving license for work and could ill afford to risk losing it.

The following day I began to feel like I should write a letter to the Chief of the Traffic Police. Whilst admitting my guilt and making no excuses for breaking the law I asked him to exercise his powers of discretion on this occasion and not to prosecute. I felt God gave me the words to use and sent the letter away. Then I waited.

Several weeks later, as I was having my evening meal, there was a knock at the front door. I opened it to two policemen who handed me a letter. They told me that there was going to be no prosecution but instead they were giving me a police caution and that would be the end of the matter. I thanked them for coming and for letting me know. However, just as they started to walk back up the drive one of them turned round and said, "You must have friends in very high places for you to get away with this offence and not be prosecuted!" We both laughed, but I was thinking I certainly did have a friend at a much higher level than either of them could imagine.

As a group we experienced God's intervention in a number of ways. We saw some people healed and some set free from demonic oppression. We were barely scratching the surface of something so rich and so expansive that it could never be exhausted or fully explored.

Naturally, seeking the Kingdom brought into focus my own employment. It raised questions not only about how I did my job but, more importantly, how did God see my job and was it of any value to Him?

The evangelical community in which I grew up placed a major emphasis on outreach and missionary endeavour. As a child I often found myself listening to stories of God's supernatural intervention on the mission field and in the lives of great missionaries of previous generations. My father would often give me biographies of missionaries which told how God had delivered them from danger and supernaturally supplied their needs in everyday practical circumstances. I was captivated by the stories of George Muller, Hudson Taylor, CT Studd, and many others. These men witnessed God's miraculous supply in amazing ways. Despite many hardships and severe difficulties there was a fullness about their lives which intrigued me. I always thought they had an inside track with God which was very different to mine and to the norm that I witnessed within Christian circles. However, I was fascinated by what God had done in their lives, and I always wanted to experience that same reality in my own life.

Also, as I have said, my parents were missionaries in Brazil. My dad had felt "called" to Brazil and in 1948, only three years after the end of the Second World War, he left Northern Ireland and arrived in Sao Paulo. He was not a member of any missionary society. Several small assemblies in the vicinity of where he had lived in Lurgan had given him their blessing and were standing with him in regards to his "calling" to Brazil. However, any funding he might receive from them was a very loose arrangement, nothing firm or regular was promised. This meant that he had no fixed visible means of income.

Nevertheless, growing up he regularly told me about cheques coming in from people he didn't know and of whom he had never heard. He was always generous with me and never seemed to have any financial concerns as far as his children were aware. He also financed and built a number of buildings to house the various assemblies in the different towns we lived in, out of his own pocket. It seemed to me that it was just natural to him that God would meet his needs.

Due to ill health, my dad came home from the mission field at the age of 86 in 1999 after spending over 50 years there. In those 50 years, he never told anyone about his financial needs and challenges or even once asked for financial help. He took all his needs and concerns directly to the Lord who proved to be more than enough for every eventuality. As a young boy I remember being quite perplexed about how this worked and thinking it was quite incredible.

With this as my background, it's natural that I also wanted to experience God in the same way as I had seen in my dad's life. I longed to experience God as those missionaries had done in bygone days. There was a very big question mark for me however. Would it be possible for me to tap into that same flow since I was just in a "regular" job? I wasn't on the mission field or in "full-time" Christian service. Indeed, I often struggled with seeing the point in my work, beyond the obvious financial benefit I received and being able to give financially into God's work.

I began to seriously ponder many of these questions and sought to understand how God viewed work. My thinking at this time was that He wasn't particularly interested in my working life beyond that I be honest and morally upright in my dealings. He was primarily interested in what I did on Sundays and in the congregation to which I belonged. I hadn't yet understood that all Christians are in "full-time Christian service," whatever their avenue of employment.

Chapter 5

Only One Envelope – No Spiritual/Secular Divide

I had now taken over the day-to-day running of the company, so how I handled the pressures and challenges in a very competitive and demanding business environment couldn't be ignored. Beyond managing a sales team, I also had to manage the company's Service and Maintenance department which offered after-sales support and breakdown cover to our customers. This was always a hassle and customers were hard to please. It was even harder to get paid.

I had always believed that "full-time Christian service" was the only way to serve God. However, here I was now spending my life working in a job with no visible "spiritual" output that I could identify. Yet I was confident that I was in the place that God wanted me to be since He had directed me so clearly. However, I felt it was a secondary, lower class calling and that I had been sidelined in some way from the real, higher class calling that my parents had experienced. I had never verbalised this but deep within I felt I had won the "booby prize." I had simply failed to make the grade.

Like many, I had a mental barrier between what was spiritual and holy and what was just ordinary, everyday life activity. I believed God primarily valued "church" related activities. However, work and earning a living, along with all other "non-spiritual" activities fell into a different category, which I thought was neutral. To my mind it didn't have much value to Him and yet it was here that I had to spend the majority of my life. The burning question of my heart became, "Am I wasting my time?" I could see that my work would be His way of providing for me in order to pay the bills and bless others along the way. Apart from that though, it wasn't of much eternal value. As a result my effort in so-called "spiritual" service within a congregational setting became my primary focus.

As Scripture says, *"You cannot serve two masters"* (Matthew 6:24) but this was in fact what I was doing. Not out of disobedience to the Lord but simply out of a practical misunderstanding of how the Kingdom operates. I was doing what Scripture says you do when you serve two masters: You love one and hate the other. God began to show me that I had an incomplete understanding of these issues.

One day, when I was doing a bit of DIY at home, Hazel came up to talk to me. She had been downstairs in the kitchen when out of the blue she felt the Lord speak to her. She said, "Thomas, I feel the Lord just said to me that your childhood had been sacrificed to Brazil and this is not what He requires of you at this time." It had never occurred to either of us that my childhood had been "sacrificed" to Brazil as, to me it had never been a sacrifice. Nevertheless, the effect on me was immediate. This was the Lord saying that it had never been His plan that I be a missionary or in so-called "full-time Christian service." He had placed me where He wanted me to be, and this was His calling on my life. Critically, I also realised that this was not some second-class afterthought due to me being disqualified or not being good enough. This brought an immediate release from an unspoken burden that I had carried for a long time.

My mindset of separating life into two camps—one spiritual, the other neutral—or even worse—secular (not of God)—was deeply ingrained in me as I think it is in the body of Christ but it is a false dichotomy.

This thinking is rooted in a profound misunderstanding of what God values and esteems as worthwhile. It is moulded by ancient Greek, pagan, Gnostic philosophy from around the second century which has influenced the church down through the centuries in very insidious ways. In simple terms, this thinking taught that the spirit world was good and the physical world was bad. Therefore, our dealings in the material, physical dimension were unclean and vulgar but the unseen, spiritual world was more noble, enlightened, and good.

The Bible dismisses this reasoning out of hand. Colossians 1:16 says, *"For in Him all things were created: things in heaven and on earth, visible and invisible, whether thrones or powers or rulers or authorities; all things have been created through Him and for Him."*

This verse places the unseen spiritual and the physical world on the same footing. Both were made through Him and both exist for Him. Also, ordinary work is part of those *"all things"* that were *"created through Him and for Him."* It is clear that work was always God's idea. He prepared the Garden of Eden for Adam in every detail. Everything was good and ready in order to provide for him so he didn't have to work in order to earn a living. That said, God still gave Adam work to do. He told him to subdue the earth and rule over it. As part of that he exercised *"authority over the fish in the sea, the birds of the air and over every living creature that moved upon the earth"* (Genesis 1:28). Adam had to name them all which I believe had a role in determining their character and disposition. From this we can see that work was very much part of God's plan even before the fall.

None other than the "prince of preachers," Charles H. Spurgeon, made this point very convincingly in a sermon in 1874:[4] He said, *"To a man who lives unto God nothing is secular, everything is sacred. He puts on his*

4 Sermon entitled "You serve the Lord" delivered on the morning of the 29th November 1874 at the Metropolitan Tabernacle. Available to read from Spurgeon's Sermons on *www.ccel.org/spurgeon*

workday garment and it is a vestment to him. He sits down to his meal and it is a sacrament. He goes forth to his labour and therein exercises the office of the priesthood. His breath is incense and his life a sacrifice. He sleeps on the bosom of God and lives and moves in the divine presence. To draw a hard and fast line and say, 'This is sacred and this is secular,' is, to my mind, diametrically opposed to the teaching of Christ and the spirit of the gospel."

As I began to see these things, I felt a new sense of purpose and clarity in what was to be my focus. I realised for the first time that my work was of value to God. Indeed, I realised my working life was the arena to which He had called me to serve Him. Neither was this a second-class calling but, in reality, it was the outworking of the *"good works which God had prepared in advance for me to walk in"* (Ephesians 2:10). He had a first-class plan for my life, and He wanted to display His power and His character through me in this "secular" environment.

The natural benefit of running a successful business is the economic benefit it imparts to the shareholders and staff and, more importantly, to its customer base via the products and services the company delivers. This in turn becomes a blessing to the economic life blood of the nation. We understand that the economies of the world *"lie in the power of the evil one"* according to 1 John 5:19. However, we also know that the heart of God in eternity was always one of recovery and redemption. Colossians 1:19-20 says, *"For God was pleased to have all His fullness dwell in Him, and through Him to reconcile to Himself all things, whether things on earth or things in heaven, by making peace through His blood, shed on the cross."* "All things" means all things, and I believe work and the nation's economy are included in that redemptive plan of God. This redemptive flow can only be worked out in the lives of His people, all of whom are called into "full-time Christian service" as they do their everyday, ordinary work in the heart of the enemy camp.

Daniel is a great example of someone who, as a civil servant, worked in the reign of a pagan king. Yet he was used to bring honour to God by the way he conducted himself. In Daniel chapter 2, after Daniel revealed the dream to Nebuchadnezzar, the king bowed down before him and acknowledged that Daniel's God was the God of all gods and Lord over all kings!

Colossians 3:23-24 was very helpful to me, *"Whatever you do, work at it with all your heart, as working for the Lord, not for human masters, since you know that you will receive an inheritance from the Lord as a reward. It is the Lord Christ you are serving"* (NIV). This is very clear, whatever you do, if done in the right attitude is seen by God as being done for Him and accepted as service to Him, and you will receive your eternal reward.

That tells me that there is no spiritual / secular dichotomy as for us nothing is secular. Now our external life converges with our internal life so we operate with a unified outlook. Now everything is "Kingdom." We have only one outlook on life, not two. We *"seek first His kingdom"* at work, at home, and at play. Of course, this gives eternal significance to our work along with every other aspect of our life.

If we lift our eyes up and see the broken world we live in, if our motivation is not just to get a pay packet at the end of the month or to climb the corporate ladder for our own benefit, our regular jobs can become a vehicle where God uses our abilities and talents to contribute to the common good of mankind in really practical ways. The welfare of those in society is enhanced when our working lives benefit those around us through the products and services we provide. Yes, it is all outworked within a commercial framework, but that is fine since a *"labourer is worthy of his hire"* (1 Timothy 5:18).

God's heart is towards mankind and we give expression to His longing to see a better world, not just in spiritual terms but also practically contributing to improving how society organises itself. After all, this is one way we can carry out the second commandment Jesus gave us, *"to love our neighbours as ourselves"* in our everyday employment. How we contribute to the benefit of humanity in our daily jobs is of fundamental value to God and, as such, is recognised as service to Him as per Colossians 3:23 and 24 above, provided it is done under His management and dependence on Him.

Let's face it, society is under great strain and who is better equipped to come up with the strategic answers needed if not those who know their God and have access to all the fountains of wisdom and knowledge that are in Christ? So, wherever we work, be it in IT, manufacturing, finance, or any other employment, we can use our talents and skills with our hearts set on being a blessing to our customer base and the wider community. In this way we can be led and used as channels of His purposes in a very needy world.

Interestingly, there is no word in the Hebrew Old Testament for "spiritual" because there was no separation in the Hebrew worldview. The totality of their lives was seen as spiritual. No part of their existence was seen as secular.

This newfound understanding taught me what was the central, pivotal point around which all these questions of "worth and eternal value" rotate. They don't rotate around the question of what is secular or what is spiritual but around one of obedience and calling. "What has the Father called *me* to do?" is the central question. Every child of God is called, and there is no such thing as a higher calling and a lesser one. The Father has no favourite children whom He deems more worthy of a higher calling than others. He is no respecter of persons. These principles apply equally to all whether you are a teacher, electrician, fireman, or whatever. All are called and set apart for God to manifest His presence and power in ordinary, everyday life. This is a very liberating and empowering truth.

It's good to see this truth becoming more recognised within certain Christian streams today. However, the outworking of it within congregational settings is still far from evident. Each child of God is called by God to use their working life as an opportunity in which He can manifest His redemptive, restoring, life-giving presence. For some it will be in our congregations or on the mission field but for the vast majority of us it will be out there in the cut and thrust of our everyday working lives right in the centre of the enemy's camp. To influence our young people into automatically assuming that "full-time Christian work" is the main route to serving God is to distort what the Kingdom is all about. I have seen it end in much frustration and disillusionment as round pegs never fit into square holes.

More than ever the workplace for many is a demanding and stressful place. Pressures to perform, produce, and succeed have never been higher. The whole "modus operandi" for many is "more bricks with less straw."[5] The Kingdom, the reign and rule of the King is the only answer to this trend. He promised, *"But seek ye first the Kingdom of God, and His righteousness; and all these things shall be added unto you"* (Matthew 6:33). This means we can count on His supply when His will, rule, and authority is at work in our lives irrespective of which career we are in.

However, I was to discover that it's one thing to know what you are called to but quite a different thing to come into the functional outworking of that calling. As we see in Scripture many of those who were called by God to undertake various tasks for Him had to undergo some radical surgery in advance of the presence of God coming on their lives, empowering them for the roles to which they were called.

Abraham, Jacob, Moses, and many others all had to go through a process that altered the basic way they functioned. This is particularly salient in

---

5 I did not coin this expression but heard it used many times by those in leadership within ICCC. This was used as a way of succinctly describing the working life in its fallen aspect where it is undertaken out of our own efforts by the "sweat of our brow." It is based on the experience of the Israelites whilst in slavery.

the story of Moses. He said to the Lord, *"... If you are pleased with me, teach me your ways. ... The Lord replied, "My Presence will go with you, and I will give you rest"* (Exodus 33:12-14 NIV). Moses wanted to know God's ways, (in other words, God's methodology) so He could go off and do the same. However, God gave Him His Presence instead and brought Moses into rest. Moses had to learn a very foundational lesson. We don't live by understanding God's ways and by implementing His precepts and principles as a formula independently from Him. Rather, we are called to walk in His Presence and enter God's rest depending on Him to make it happen.

I didn't understand any of that at the time as I was still functioning from the perspective that success was down to me. All that I was doing was still the result of my own effort and my own ability. God hadn't finished with me though and He began positioning me so that He could bring me into a new understanding of His ways. I was soon to discover that work, in His economy, was to be characterised by rest.

Chapter 6

Between a Rock and a Hard Place

Now that I understood that my daily work was the avenue of service to which God had called me, I naturally started to pray and seek His will and guidance in all the various facets of managing the business. I was earnestly doing everything I knew to do to include God in my everyday decisions. Having said that though, my basic approach was still that it was up to me to make everything happen. I was very much operating from a self-resourced, self-reliant mindset. Instinctively, however, I knew I was only scratching the surface of what this walk of faith could look like, and I eagerly sought to understand how it could be fully outworked in my life.

My desire to see His power at work in my life intensified, and the verse I quoted earlier was a constant challenge to me: *"The kingdom of God is not in words but in power"* (1 Corinthians 4:20). I saw this as God saying His power would be manifest where His will and His ways were in operation. The opposite must also be true. If His power is not being manifest, then it must be because His will and methods of operating are not being put to work.

Although my desire exceeded my understanding of how this Kingdom operates, He encouraged me with some small victories along the way. I remember very clearly an incident that happened around this time. One of my most important customers asked for help. He used a competitor's brand of press brakes so, due to his large number of existing machines, he was unwilling to start buying my brand. Nevertheless, he knew that our after-sales service was good so, due to budgetary constraints on a certain contract, he asked if I could supply him with a secondhand machine of the brand he was using. I saw no reason not to help him.

I checked out my contacts in the second-hand market in England and found a machine that came within his budget, to the specification he required. He agreed to buy it so I went over to England to inspect the machine and ensure that it was working and in the condition and specification as described. I had to pay for the machine on collection but wouldn't get paid until it was delivered installed and operating. In due course we delivered the machine, installed and commissioned it, leaving the customer to work it for a few days before payment was due.

The following day, I received a call saying it had broken down. My engineer went out and was able to identify and repair the fault. The customer started to use it again but early next morning I received another call saying it had broken down again. Our engineer went back, found a different fault and got it running again. This continued off and on for a couple of weeks, and my customer became very frustrated as he was now falling behind on his commitments to his own customer.

Eventually he called me in for a meeting saying he couldn't continue with this and asked what I was going to do about it. I promised to pay for a specialist engineer to come over from the manufacturer of this particular brand to give it a complete overhaul and ensure that any faults were addressed satisfactorily. He accepted my proposal but made it clear that if this didn't work he would have to return the machine as he couldn't accept such low levels of reliability.

Such an outcome would have serious repercussions for me as not only was I out of pocket for the cost of the machine but it was also costing me a lot for the backup I was having to provide. Furthermore, if I did have to take the machine back, what could I do with it? The company

I bought it from wouldn't want it and, as it wasn't my usual brand of machine, I would find it difficult to sell to another customer, assuming I could get it to operate reliably again. However, I had no choice but to agree to my customer's terms.

On that basis the manufacturer's engineer came over and spent two or three days working on the machine, testing it thoroughly, so, when he left, I was feeling confident that all would be well.

After lunch the following day I received that dreaded call again telling me the machine had broken down. I was now in serious trouble! I rang one of my engineers and arranged to meet him at the customer's premises within the hour. When I arrived the customer was most upset and demanded I get "… bleep … bleep … that heap of junk …" out of his workshop! I went down to the machine promising to come back up to his office once I had checked it out. I hoped that the operator had done something stupid or there was some other simple explanation for this latest fault.

My engineer began his normal checks but after a while it became clear that he wasn't making any progress so, since he had to get back to the customer he had been with previously, we decided there was no point in continuing.

It was now nearly 5:00 p.m. All the other machine operators had left for the day and I was alone in the large workshop. There was an eerie silence as I stood and pondered my options. I was feeling frustrated and annoyed for getting myself into this predicament but here I was, stuck and feeling vulnerable and very much out of ideas as to what I could do next.

Standing there in the silence, I wondered where was God in all this. Was He not interested in what I was facing? Would He intervene and save me? I had no idea how He could, even if He was willing. A verse then came into my mind. It was Psalm 46:1, and I spoke it out loud to myself, *"God is our refuge and strength, a very present help in trouble. Therefore I will not fear ..."*! Quoting this out loud several times made this truth seem very real to me, and it affected how I was feeling inside. Was I not in trouble? Could I depend then on His help? This brought everything I felt God had been teaching me down to one simple, basic element. Was what I had just words, or could I see the power of His Kingdom working in these very real circumstances in which I now found myself?

I was certainly in trouble. This was going to cost me over £40,000 if I had to take the machine out which, even by today's standards, is a sizeable amount. As I stood there, I felt I was standing between a rock and a hard place. I was face to face with what I believed were two realities—one in the physical and one in the spiritual dimension. On the one hand the broken-down machine, on the other, God's Word promising help. In myself I could not change anything but somehow, I knew that this was an opportunity to learn more how I could put these spiritual realities to work.

I started to pray. I reminded God of His Word, that He had said He was a very real help in trouble, and I told Him now would be a really good opportunity to see His help in action. I then remembered that verse in Mark 11 where we are told to *"speak to the mountain"* and *"command it to be lifted up and cast into the sea."* Although on the one hand I felt I was being foolish and very naive, on the other, I knew Jesus had commanded His disciples to do just that. So I tentatively began to speak to the machine and commanded it to be repaired. I commanded that it would work perfectly from that day onwards.

Now I was going to have to switch the machine on which caused me to feel even more foolish. If anyone had seen me or heard me, they would surely be locking me up in a mental institution. What was I thinking? I went to the main electrical cabinet and switched on the machine.

The CNC controls came to life with flashing lights and all the usual alarms operating although that had all been operating previously. The proof was in pressing the operator foot pedal. I pressed it and nothing happened. The machine still wasn't working so I switched it off again.

My heart sank and I felt deflated, but I just couldn't give up and walk away. I knew God was real and His Word was real, and it promised that He was a very present help in trouble, no qualifications, no "ifs" or "maybes." Besides, if I gave up now, I felt like it would damage my confidence in God and my ability to trust Him to work in my everyday circumstances. I couldn't risk that so I had to see this through!

I looked to the Lord again and wondered what to do next. I waited a few minutes and felt led to look around the electrical cabinet. Even though I wasn't an electrician there might be something obvious I could detect. As I did that I noticed a small metal box, no more than a couple of inches square, at the top of the control cabinet which I opened. I found six fused connections inside which I checked and found one which was blown. There were several good fuses lying at the bottom of the cabinet so I replaced it, closed the cabinet door, switched the electrical power back on, pressed the foot pedal and the machine worked!

I operated the machine for several minutes as I could hardly believe it was now functioning and then went back up to the office to speak to the customer. I explained to him about the fuse and that I was now confident the machine was okay. He understood a blown fuse wasn't a big issue and thanked me for my help and for being so responsive. He promised that if the machine worked without any more faults for the next two weeks he would make payment in full. I swallowed hard, really wanting to ask him to pay me sooner in case any more faults developed, but in whom was I trusting? So I shook his hand and told him to pay me whenever he was happy with the machine. The machine worked from that point on, and I received payment in full two or three weeks later.

Afterwards, naturally, I wondered what had happened here. It was clearly not just a simple fuse that had caused all of the trouble. During the previous repairs no fuses had been found to be defective and there had been many different faults. So what happened? I don't know! All I know is that, despite my foolish naivety, if I had done the natural, logical thing, I would have ended up taking the machine out. Graciously the Lord directed me to what was wrong at that particular time. My dependence on Him was vindicated. He orchestrated events to ensure I was delivered and, as far as I was concerned, that was all that mattered.

Chapter 7

Discovering the Blockage

I mentioned earlier that God was positioning me to understand that work, in His economy, is to be characterised by rest. At the start of 1992 I attended a conference in England, hosted by the International Christian Chamber of Commerce (ICCC) which was founded by a Swedish businessman called Gunner Olsen. Gunner felt God had called him to the marketplace and to use his own business as a vehicle to glorify God. As a result of his remarkable experiences and what the Lord taught him, he was led to found ICCC. It majored on teaching that there is no spiritual / secular divide and that the call to the marketplace is, in fact, a first-class calling. It also emphasised the importance of what it means to walk by faith in the marketplace. It sounded a call to business leaders to hand their businesses and their working lives over to the Lord and learn to walk in dependence on Him and see a release of God's presence and power through their working lives.

As I was getting ready to attend the first session of the conference that Friday evening, unexpectedly, God brought back to my mind a scene which happened regularly when I was a boy in Brazil, living in the small town of Rio Pardo. Most nights, after our evening meal, there would be a gentle tap on our back door. My mother would open it to a small boy who could not have been more than 7 or 8 years old. He was in his bare feet, his clothes were torn and dirty, and he would hand an old, empty tin can to my mother which she would fill with all the meal leftovers. We were told these scraps of food were to feed his family's pigs and chickens, but we suspected it was actually to feed the family as well, so mum would usually give him something extra to take home.

I hadn't thought about this in years but for some reason it all came flooding back to me so vividly as I walked into the large room where the first session of the conference was to be held. As I sat down, the Lord impressed upon me that He saw me as that little child. I was poor and malnourished, my clothes were dirty and torn, and that tin can full of scraps was how He saw all that I was doing and producing in my life. It seemed that all my hard work and diligent effort trying to make the grade and please Him, in His eyes, wasn't worth a hill of beans.

This was so strong and real to me that I was quite shocked by it! In the natural I thought things were going well. The family and business aspects of my life were good, and I was doing as much as the next guy, if not more, as far as attending to the spiritual aspects of my life.

However, now God was graciously lifting the curtain and allowing me to see myself and all I was producing in my life from His perspective. How could it be that all my hard work and strained effort and diligence over the years, in both the spiritual aspects of my life as well as my job, family life, and congregational input were just like this dirty tin can filled with scraps of food? How could all my best efforts amount to so little? I was shocked by the realisation that God saw me as that unkempt, impoverished, malnourished little child.

I didn't connect this at the time with those verses in Revelation 3 where the exact same scenario takes place. The same veil is removed in the letter to the New Testament Laodicean church. They are told, *"You do not realize that you are wretched, pitiful, poor, blind and naked"* (Revelation 3:17 NIV).

I really didn't know what to make of this or how to respond but felt very deflated and concerned. If this was the Lord speaking, then He would have to make it clear over the course of the weekend where and how I had missed it so very badly.

As I went to bed that night and thought over my life, I became convicted by what God had said but I couldn't understand how I could have done anything differently. Surely everyone I knew lived from the same basic premise I had done. I had been pushing hard for years, day in and day out trying my best to keep all the various plates in my life spinning. Now I didn't feel I had much more left to give. I had assumed this was the way life had to be lived. Yes, I prayed and sought God's help but surely it was me who had to make things happen. I had to push my hardest to succeed as best I could. I had applied this mindset to every aspect of my life, including my spiritual walk. I thought that was the way every good Christian lived.

The teaching that weekend was to show me where I had gone wrong. The main topic centred around entering God's rest. The speaker talked about Hebrews 4 which promises that there remains today a rest for God's people. It then goes on to counsel us not to come short or to miss out on that rest. It draws a parallel between the promise to the nation of Israel to enter the promised land and us, as New Testament believers, entering into God's rest today. It then warns us that the children of Israel missed it because they didn't mix the message they heard with faith. This verse then jumped out at me with blinding force: *"For he that is entered into His rest, he also hath ceased from his own works, as God did from His"* (Hebrews 4:10).

The speaker addressed the central issue of self-reliance and living from our own efforts and resources. He showed from Scripture how God sees "self-resourced" living and dependence on "Self" as sin. Jeremiah makes this crystal clear, *"This is what the Lord says: 'Cursed is the one who trusts in man, who draws strength from mere flesh and whose heart turns away from the Lord. That person will be like a bush in the wastelands; they will not see prosperity when it comes. They will dwell in the parched places of the desert, in a salt land where no one lives. But blessed is the one who trusts in the Lord, whose confidence is in Him. They will be like a tree planted by the water that sends out its roots by the stream. It does not fear when heat comes; its leaves are always green. It has no worries in a year of drought and never fails to bear fruit"* (Jeremiah 17:5-8 NIV).

What an amazing picture of fruitfulness for those who abandon the self-dependent, self-resourced life. On the contrary, what an arid and dry picture is painted of life lived in "a salt land" by our own efforts and with this I could very much identify.

It began to dawn on me that life, from God's perspective, was to be lived from an entirely different basis to how I had been living mine. Operating out of my own resources, living out of self-effort and self-reliance was not God's way. I began to understand why, from God's perspective, my life to that point had amounted to so little.

This was all shocking to me but also extraordinary. I saw that here was the promise, if I could only grasp the nuts and bolts of how it worked, which would lead me into the life I had been searching for since that night back at Spring Harvest when Floyd McClung had challenged me about *"living beyond the level of my own ability."* I saw that this "rest" brings self-resourced, self-reliance to an end so that we *"cease from our own works, as God did from His"* on the seventh day of creation.

We had the Saturday afternoon free so I decided to spend it alone to consider all these new insights. As I did that, the Holy Spirit began to show me the central role that faith must play in our lives. He brought several Scriptures to mind which made faith an absolute imperative if we were to please God. For example, Romans 1:17: *"The just shall live by faith."* This is not talking about saving faith but a foundational, ongoing dependence from which we live our lives. *"But without faith it is impossible to please Him"* (Hebrews 11:6), came to me with great clarity. These verses made a convincing case of course, but when I saw what John had to say about it, I became truly convicted by how I had been living.

The people came to Jesus and asked Him, *"What shall we do, that we might work the works of God?"* Jesus replied to them, *"This is the work of God, that ye believe on Him whom He hath sent"* (John 6:28-29). The Greek word for "believe" is the same as for "faith" but in English we use the word "faith" as the noun and "believe" as the verb.

Of course, this radically contrasted with how I had been living. It also raised another problem. I saw that to live by faith, by definition, means that we can no longer live from a self-resourced and self-reliant posture. To put it the other way, self-effort is, in fact, a by-product of self-reliance or faith in "Self." Dependence on God and dependence on "Self" are mutually exclusive! That seems completely obvious to me now but it wasn't then. In other words, biblical faith is only activated when we stop depending on ourselves. Faith here is the flip side of the surrender coin! It is only as we surrender that faith is activated. I saw that we have not been given a long list of things we need to do as Christians. There is only one work we have been given to do and that is to believe. *"The work of God is to believe on Him."* Not as a one-off experience but a continual daily posture. This means our obedience is not an obedience of works and effort but an obedience of faith. I was stunned to realise that as a Christian, the sum total of our walk is believing. This was such a stark contrast to how I had been living. I realised that operating as I had been was to produce "dead works."

However, there was another difficult pill I had to swallow and this one was the hardest for me to accept! I realised that if we are to live by faith and dependence on someone else, then, by definition, we must give up control. In a flash I saw the stark reality I was now facing. Control was the key issue! My understanding of surrender to this point had been very shallow indeed. To enter God's rest called for something much deeper. It wasn't so much related to the surrender of external things or even giving up my own will and desires. I had done that many times before. This now challenged my very right to be in control of myself.

I have since learnt that giving up control is the point where a profound change starts to happen. This is the only way we can take His yoke upon us.[6] To take His yoke is to place ourselves where we are no longer in control and have come under His yoke and His control. This is how we enter the "rest" Jesus talked about in that passage. As Christians we have asked the Lord to come into our lives but, for some of us, it's as if He has come in as a guest and we offer Him the guest bedroom while we retain the care and control over the rest of the house. In effect, to continue with the analogy, that day the Lord was asking me to hand the keys of my entire house over to Him. He was asking me to sign the deed over to Him so that He would become the proprietor. He was asking me to give up ownership of my life entirely.

A practical example of what it means to give up control might help. Take a lifeguard swimming out to rescue someone who is drowning. He knows if the person is still fighting and trying desperately to save himself he is a risk to them both. A trained lifeguard will wait until he is given consent or the person, out of exhaustion, stops trying to save themselves. This is the line in the sand that allows a very real exchange to take place. The person who is drowning entrusts himself entirely into the charge, resources and abilities of the lifeguard. He trusts that the lifeguard is capable of bringing him ashore and from then on, he stops his struggling. He "ceases from His own work" and "rests" yielding himself up into the life-saving abilities of the lifeguard.

A surrender that has not crossed this line has not yet given Christ effective control. We may have given up our own ambitions and our wills at some level but we are still, in effect, in "self"-management

---

6 Matthew 11:30

mode, living out of our own strength, abilities and resources. That day, I felt the Lord directly challenging me to take myself out of my own hands and give myself unreservedly over into His keeping and management alone.

We resist what we do not know or understand. However, that Saturday afternoon my eyes were being opened to see Christ for all He wanted to be to me. This was not something negative, it was the best possible news, and it put surrendering into a completely different perspective. It transformed my previously grudging response, where my fingers would have had to be prised open in order to get me to release control into something I gladly and wholeheartedly wanted to run towards in glad abandon.

I didn't realise it at the time, but I was to discover that this is the key that unlocks the dungeon, allowing us to walk free into the warm sunshine of our Father's inheritance. This was choosing to exchange my own feeble resources for the vast, infinite riches that are Christ. The Father was indeed drawing me to the place someone has described as, *"the end of 'Self' is the beginning of Christ."*[7]

---

7 Quote from http://christian-quotes.achristian.com/Consecreation-Quotes

Chapter 8

Removing the Blockage

The Sunday morning session of the conference started with worship and then we were asked to make ourselves comfortable so we could be still and wait on God, resting quietly in His presence. As I settled myself in the quietness, I began to think about the amazing insight I had received about rest. I knew this was what I wanted and desperately needed. By now I was deeply convicted by the futility of my own efforts and utterly convinced that, *"Unless the LORD builds the house, They labor in vain who build it; Unless the LORD guards the city, The watchman keeps awake in vain. It is vain for you to rise early, To retire late, To eat the bread of anxious labours—For He gives [blessings] to His beloved even in his sleep"* (Psalms 127:1-2 AMPC).

I'd had my fill of *"rising up early and retiring late and eating the bread of anxious toil."* I simply couldn't go back to my old ways of striving and straining and living by the "sweat of my brow." I just knew He would have to break that pattern in my life. I knew what I needed to do, but the thought of giving up control of myself made me feel very vulnerable indeed. I felt like I was being asked to jump off the edge of a very high cliff without a parachute or a safety net below. It meant finding myself in free fall, beyond my ability to save myself. I understood this was putting myself in a place where I would no longer be in control of outcomes. The big question was, could I be sure He would catch me?

Choosing to accept the invitation of Jesus and put on His yoke and enter His rest felt to me like I was choosing helplessness. That made me feel uncomfortable but it shouldn't have surprised me. Hadn't Jesus said a prerequisite to seeing the Kingdom outworked in our lives was to become like a little child? *"Whoever does not accept and receive and welcome the Kingdom of God like a little child [does] shall not in any way enter it [at all]"* (Luke 18:17 AMPC). The key characteristic of a child is total dependence. Children have no concept of having to provide for themselves; instead, they have a confidence that their parents will see to everything. Nevertheless, I felt vulnerable, exposed, and unsure of what to do next. I was deeply concerned and wondering how this would all work out in practice.

I then got the feeling that someone had moved very close beside me. I opened my eyes and was surprised to find that there was no one there. As I closed my eyes again I realised something was happening which I couldn't understand. It felt like an inward thing but yet it seemed to be outside of me as well. I became aware of what I instinctively realised was the presence of Christ Himself. Not physically, of course, but He might as well have been, He was just as real. I sensed He was being considerate and gentle in His approach. On the other hand, He was inviting me to unreservedly release myself into His management. I instinctively knew that He would never force me; it had to be a voluntary act on my part, and He would utterly respect my decision, whatever I chose. The options for me were now crystal clear, I could give myself up and release myself entirely into His keeping, like that drowning person who rests in the arms of the lifeguard, or I could choose to play it "safe" and stay in control, living by my own efforts as I had been doing. It was up to me!

Inside, I knew that I could no longer carry this little tin can I had tried so hard to fill. I had enough of trying to fill it with all my self-generated activities and my self-reliant scraps. It all seemed repugnant to me now. I'm not sure what words I said but inside my heart leapt as I so wanted to yield myself and everything else up to Him.

As I did so I found myself being enveloped, no, I was overwhelmed by the reality of His gentle, loving presence. I was overcome by the realisation that He was Love and that He utterly and totally loved *me*. He loved me just as I was, without qualification, without exception, and without limitation. I realised that He was seeking my consent to come and take possession of all that I was. I could not resist this love, nor did I want to. I just had to yield myself entirely to Him. All sense of caution and self-preservation was thrown to the wind as I abandoned myself to Him unreservedly and absolutely. All those areas of my life where I had striven so hard to please God, my desire to serve Him, my care for my family, my work and finances, I now released into His management and control. All I wanted to do was to become fully yielded and fully surrendered to the immediacy of His gentle, loving embrace. How could I deny Him? His sweet presence and gentle influences released me from all my fear. I welcomed Him without restraint as His loving presence began to take possession within, flooding every part of my consciousness with Himself. He was a blanket of personified love wrapping Himself around me inside and out.

Something then broke in me. The basis of all my striving, my self-reliance and self-effort crumbled. All my pressures and anxieties drained away and, inwardly, I knew that He had taken possession. The last traces of seeing God as that hard, demanding judge who was just waiting to pounce on me if I stepped out of line were washed away. I saw that He was extraordinarily, indescribably, infinitely good. He let me see His heart, and I saw there was no anger or judgement there. There was no condemnation, no accusing finger, just a longing to do me good and shower His love upon me. I saw that He earnestly wanted to rescue and recover me from all my brokenness. His love for me was real, not something fragile or fickle but a stable, robust love that was strong enough to handle my brokenness. It was something I could rest and depend on every day of my life. Peace—a deep, thick, velvet blanket of peace—enveloped me, the likes of which I had never before experienced. I was lost in His loving embrace as the deepest recesses of my being were occupied by the divine Presence.

After some time, someone in the room started reading from Song of Solomon chapter 2. I felt the Lord whispered the words to me personally.

"He brought me into the banqueting house and His banner over me is love." This spoke to me of the new reality I had entered into. *"His left Hand is under my head and His right arm embraces me."* This revealed His desire to be intimate with me, not to be harsh or hard but the exact opposite—to do me good, to show me His love. I sensed, going forward, that He wanted us to simply commune together with no ulterior motive on my part. With me not always coming and asking for this and that and then rushing away but simply drawing near for His own sake, no agenda, just to know Him and to enjoy Him and to love Him.

"Lo, the winter is past, the rain is over and gone: the flowers appear on the earth, the singing of birds is come, and the voice of the turtle is heard in the land." This promised a new level of fruitfulness and abundance and the reality of living in a continual season of *"springtime."*

Travelling home that Sunday afternoon I was overcome by what had happened. This was not a figment of my imagination or some random, emotional experience that I would wake up from the next day. This was not religion. This was the Almighty Father drawing near in heartfelt love to His child, caressing all my fears and struggles away. It was the river of His delights flowing over my bruised and wounded heart with healing and restoration. It went beyond my highest expectation and my deepest longing. Nothing could have prepared me for the overwhelming tide of contentment and peace which engulfed me. That verse in Ephesians 3:19 that had tantalised me for so many years promising I could *"be filled (through all your being) unto all the fullness of God (may have the richest measure of the divine Presence, and become a body wholly filled and flooded with God Himself)"* (Ephesians 3:19 AMPC), had now become my wonderful reality. I couldn't get over what had happened, and I still haven't, nor do I ever want to. I could not digest the implications of what had happened or predict the changes this would bring.

Over the following weeks several well-known verses began to come to me but now they seemed to take on an entirely different perspective. One was John 14:23 when *"Jesus answered, If a person really loves Me, He will keep My word; and My Father will love him, and We will come to Him and make our home [abode, special dwelling place] with Him"* (AMPC). Here, our attention is turned inwards to the central truth that Christianity, at its very core, carries the promise that we can experience and enjoy the presence of the Father and the Son within, in a real, loving, and tangible life-transforming way. I had on occasion been aware of this inner presence over the years and especially so since my experience with the Lord at Spring Harvest '83. However, it was usually during prolonged times of prayer and fasting or in worship at some conference or other, but it had not been the norm. I found it to be illusive, intermittent, and sporadic. I had found it impossible to maintain in my day-to-day life and, wrongly, I always felt that its absence was because I hadn't done enough or hadn't taken enough time with Him. This was now very different. There was a wonderful, effortless constancy about this. I was continually aware of His loving presence. I kept expecting this to dim and perhaps even wear off but that didn't happen and hasn't happened even after all these years. Sure, there have been fluctuations in the intensity of it, but I know He will never leave me! Faith has become substance.

That hunger that came into my life after Spring Harvest, which was like a deep yearning, restless void was not just filled but now overflowed. The days when I looked outside myself seeking to make contact with an external, divine being had ended. Now I simply had to look within to encounter Him in a vital way. Indeed, I felt an entirely new dimension of reality had opened up to me. I described it at the time like an internal set of invisible doors, which I hadn't realised were there, suddenly being flung wide open, allowing me to see into an entirely new dimension. This, of course, is speaking of the spirit realm, the reality of the Holy of Holies now opened up within us. Andrew Murray said, *"The mystic insists especially on the truth that the organ by which God is to be known is not the understanding, but by the heart; Only love can know God in truth."*[8]

I mentioned earlier how the Lord confronted me as He had the Laodicean Christians in Revelation chapter 3 about them being *"wretched, pitiful, poor, blind and naked."* Now He had brought me into the most amazing reality of what verse 20 describes: *"Behold, I stand at the door and knock: if any man hear my voice, and open the door, I will come in to him, and will sup with him, and he with me."* By yielding up control I had opened the door for Him to come in to me and reside in me as He never had before. I love the thought that is being communicated by that word "sup." Thayer's Greek Lexicon[9] describes it as, *"I will make him to share in my most intimate and blissful contact."* I discovered that time spent in fellowship with Him was now on an entirely different level. It was enough to simply rest with Him and drink from this inner well, this fountain of life.

Jesus promised his poor disciples, *"I will not leave you as orphans; I will come to you"* (John 14:18 NIV). The term "orphan" perfectly described my life up to this point. My characteristic attitude and thinking prior to this was from the standpoint that it was all down to me to make things happen. I had seen "Lordship" as another demand which I needed to satisfy out of my own resources but now the tables were reversed.

He had me in His hands and I was under His care and management and that was a wonderful release. I was no longer an orphan and I was no longer alone. He, in the fullness and richness of all that He

---

8 Andrew Murray, prolific author and missionary to South Africa in the 19th century. Quote from "Introduction" chapter of his little book "Wholly for God," page 23. Don't let the word "mystic" put you off. It is defined as someone who believes in the existence of realities beyond human comprehension. How can anyone accept New Testament Christianity and not fulfil that criteria?
9 Thayer's Greek Lexicon by Publisher Harper & Brothers, Author *Joseph Henry Thayer*

is in Himself, had come to me and taken me into Himself. What an astounding thing to say! I could hardly believe it. I was overcome by His amazing condescension.

Chapter 9

The "Self-Life"

I have shared my own story to this point because I hope it will resonate with many believers who are struggling and hungry, searching for more. They have experienced forgiveness and the assurance of Heaven but have not discovered the abundant "Spirit-filled" life the New Testament promises. I want to share what the blockage was which had prevented me from entering into the fullness of God's provision.

This is where we must define what is meant by these biblical terms "Flesh," "Self," or the "Old Self". We need a clear and functional understanding of them if we are to recognise when we are "walking in the flesh" or "walking in the Spirit."

My understanding of what had actually happened to me began to fall into place once I saw the central exchange that occurred, not just when satan rebelled but also when Adam fell.

Isaiah 14:13-14 gives us an insight into satan's motivation. "*You said in your heart, 'I will ascend to the heavens; I will raise my throne above the stars of God; I will sit enthroned on the mount of assembly, on the utmost heights of Mount Zaphon. I will ascend above the tops of the clouds; I will make myself like the Most High*" (NIV). Here, we see satan, in effect, usurping control and separating himself from his maker—his source. He was setting up a rival will to God's benevolent will and stepping away from God's original design. We see that his actions were first and foremost a declaration of independence and self-reliant self-rule.

The central characteristic which satan demonstrates as he outlines his ambition of independence is not just that he is pursuing his own will and objectives but, most importantly, he is also egotistically now to be the source and the means through which he will accomplish those objectives. He is the one who is going to make it all happen. *"I will ascend to the heavens; I will raise my throne ... I will sit enthroned ... I will ascend above the tops of the clouds; I will make myself like the Most High."* Those are very telling statements!

This is a quantum shift away from the divinely established order. It was not just a rejection of God's order but a rejection of His provision and supply as well. It was an astonishing manifesto of autonomous, self-resourced self-reliance.

Then we see the exact same thing played out when Adam fell. The Garden of Eden was a divine ecosystem.[10] Adam awakened to an environment where everything he might need or desire was already freely provided for his enjoyment and satisfaction. He didn't have to earn his keep or contribute to his sustenance in any way. He had a job to do for sure but not in order to support himself or provide for himself.

A loving creator must surely carry the responsibility for providing and catering for the ongoing provision, wellbeing, and sustenance of those He has created. How could love do otherwise? God saw to it that his every need was abundantly supplied and everything He prepared was good. He said so six times in Genesis so it must all have been very good indeed. We see also that the divine presence was Adam's daily experience as he was able to interact freely with God. This was all the result of God's loving intention and detailed, deliberate design.

This is the context then within which we must interpret Adam's actions. The temptation satan used to persuade Adam to eat of the fruit of the tree was the promise of independence. He said, *"Ye shall be as gods,*

---

10 Gunner Olsen used this expression in a recent ICCC meeting. It reflects the all-encompassing dimension in which Adam lived under God's infinite care and provision in the Garden. Gunner then went on to apply this same expression as an analogy to the Kingdom of God.

knowing good and evil" (Genesis 3:5). In effect, the same motivation as satan when he rebelled. This was enticing Adam to buy into satan's manifesto of autonomous, self-resourced self-reliance. This caused Adam to reject God's established order and his role within it, choosing to take himself into his own hands, activating his own will for the first time. In effect, Adam deliberately chose to step out of a life of dependence on God's order and His provision and stepped into independent "Self," into "Self"-reliance and "Self"-resourced living. Adam not only forfeited fellowship with his Creator, but he lost his provision and supply as well.

God had breathed His breath of life into Adam at his awakening. Now, however, although his spirit would remain alive, as it was immortal, it was severed from its home source. Adam terminated his life which was based on rest (i.e., dependence on a source outside himself), and exchanged it for a life of dependence on "Self." On the day he ate the fruit, he died. In other words, he voluntarily and deliberately unplugged himself from his internal, divine wellspring. He separated himself from his Creator and sustainer and stepped away from God's provision, favour, and blessing into an entirely new regime—an independent regime where everything would now depend on his ability and his performance. He would be independent but totally alone. There would be no one to help him, no internal or external means of support.

This awakening of Adam's independent "Self" placed "Self" now as his fixed centre rather than God, as it had once been. This reality now forced Adam to operate exclusively from the meagre resources at his disposal within "Self." From this point on he lived by the *"sweat of his brow" "in sorrow and toil."* Is that not so utterly familiar to us today? I wonder how he felt when it dawned on him what he had done! The realisation that he had turned his back on his Father's loving ecosystem and His vast unlimited resources, exchanging them for what he could generate out of his own puny effort, must have been a savage and devastating blow!

This separation from his divine source also meant that he now operated under the illusion that he could act as a god, functioning in independence out of his own initiative for his own ends. He now saw himself as a "god," that is, as a self-generating, self-resourced, and self-reliant being who was, in effect, an autonomous, self-sufficient entity. This is the central deception that enveloped mankind as a result of the fall, and it is the very essence of "Self." It ignores the truth that we are created beings so dependency was a basic function of our design and operation from the outset. We can only ever be derivative beings; we are not independent as we will see.

When Adam unplugged himself from his divine connection and followed satan's lead he unknowingly allowed satan to take over that inner spirit connection which had previously connected him to his Creator. In effect, satan gained access to Adam's "Self", taking control so that Adam would become a captive to the power of satan. He became a slave to sin and, as such, satan's subject locked into operating under the laws of the kingdom of darkness. This is clear from many Scriptures. For example, 1 John 3:7 states *"He who commits sin, who practices evildoing, is of the devil, takes his character from the evil one"* (AMPC) and Acts 26:18, *"... to open their eyes and turn them from darkness to light, and from the power of satan to God"* (NIV). We see the same truth expressed in Ephesians 2:2, *"You were obedient to and under the control of the demon spirit that still constantly works in the sons of disobedience"* (AMPC).

Adam clearly had no idea this "control" was the very thing satan had been seeking all along. Naively, under the serpent's influence, he had been deceived into thinking that it would be better for him to become autonomous and to live out of his own "self"-generated resources. Adam was now responsible for navigating his life out of his own definition of good and evil. However, now he is turned inwards with a self-centred, self-reliant focus. Making choices, yes, but not in freedom. Choices predicated on "Self" as his priority, the opposite to what he had previously known. It placed "Self" rather than God as his core motivation, his *raison d'être* for all he was, for all he did, and for all he would become. The very purpose of his life was now turned inwards, centred on "Self" which became the dominant, driving force of his being.

This explains why humanity today operates from the same deluded "Self" perspective, thinking itself to be in control and independent, capable of operating out of its own resources for its own ends but unaware these are the very traits that evidence all is under satan's dominium and control.

All of this helps us define in a functional way what the Bible is referring to when using the term "flesh," "self," or our "old self." It is referring to that autonomous, egocentric, self-resourced, self-reliant mindset. Essentially, it is that independent disposition where we act out of our own sense of self-competence, living by our own efforts for our own ends. It also carries the thought of "being of the five senses" where we use our "senses" to gain knowledge to make it in life.

This is the true nature and character of "Self"and explains why this mindset is the enemy within. We don't consciously choose to operate this way; it is simply the context within which we were born and from which we function.

This is our root problem: "Self" is under the jurisdiction of the kingdom of darkness and locked into operating under the "law of sin and death." It has set itself up as a parallel source, operating from a deluded sense of independence set in continual, fixed opposition to God's original design, will, and intention.

To put this succinctly, the central sin of humanity as described in the early chapters of Genesis is that we have all followed in Adam's footsteps. He turned away from reliance and dependence on his original source, away from his loving, self-giving Father and turned to a rival source. We in turn have followed suit and drawn our supply from the well of our own deluded sense of independence and autonomous, self-willed, self-reliance which, as we said, is a by-product of satan's operating system running within.

We can see, therefore, for "Self" to be in control is in effect for us to live in hostility and opposition to God irrespective of whether we are Christians or not. We see this clearly stated in Romans 8. *"The mind governed by the flesh is death* (separation from God), *but the mind governed by the Spirit is life and peace. The mind governed by the flesh is hostile to God; it does not submit to God's law, nor can it do so. Those who are in the realm of the flesh cannot please God"* (Romans 8:6-8 NIV— parenthesis mine). This verse makes it pretty clear. As Christians, we can live *"governed"* by "Self" or *"governed"* by the "Holy Spirit." This raises the central question we need to ask ourselves: Which source are we depending on to make it in life?

Of course, the critical point to recognise is that to be dependent on either source is to be submitted to that source and therefore "governed" by it!

Importantly, "Self" is not to be understood simply as some intangible dark force that sits on our shoulders seeking to trip us up into negative and destructive behaviour. No indeed! "Self" is just as capable of doing what, on the surface, looks like "good deeds" as it is of doing "evil deeds." Remember, Adam fell by eating of the tree of *"the knowledge of good and evil."* This means we cannot judge merely by how our actions appear on the surface; we need to identify their source.

There is much evidence of this as we look around the world today. Many who deny the existence of God devote their lives to "good causes," selflessly relieving pain and suffering in some of the most deprived areas of the world. Nevertheless, the point has been convincingly made that from God's perspective, all that originates from "Self" is unacceptable. Even our very best righteous acts, in God's eyes, *"are filthy rags"* (Isaiah 64:6). We know that doesn't change when we are born again according to Romans 7:18 where Paul confessed *"For I know that in me (that is, in my flesh) dwelleth no good thing."* That is because, no matter what "Self" produces, whether on the surface it appears what we might describe as "good apples" or perhaps "bad apples" in God's eyes, they are all still apples and not pears to use that analogy. Good and bad apples are produced but both are the product of something rooted in independence and separation from God and opposition to God.

This is the "modus operandi" we were born with. In effect, it is our enemy's default rogue operating system running within. This explains the cold nature of the alienation and separation which "Self" experiences today as a result of the fall. It gives context to our crippling, fear-inducing, orphaned reality. We believe that we are alone in an unpredictable, dangerous world doing our level best to mitigate the negatives, searching for whatever positives we can find. However, inside, even though many don't know what is wrong, nothing quite fills the void of our isolation and separation from our Father's house or relieves that daily grinding reality of having to face life's challenges alone out of our own meagre resources. That is the epitome of what it means to live as an orphan!

This independent, "Self" disposition is the source of our dysfunctional brokenness even as Christians. To live from "Self" as a Christian is to live "*like a bush in the wastelands. ... They will dwell in the parched places of the desert, in a salt land where no one lives*" (Jeremiah 17:5-8 NIV). This is to live as an orphan separated from our Father's provision, living outside the garden of His provision and delights. It is to be burdened with the weight of sustaining ourselves and trying to keep ourselves safe.

Jesus said, "*If any man will come after me, let him deny himself*" (Luke 9:23). He didn't differentiate between good "Self" and bad "Self' as some appear to do. He is saying the central requirement to follow Jesus is that we no longer live our lives depending on "Self," that is, operating out of that autonomous, self-resourced, self-reliant mindset!

There is only one way out of this predicament as "Self" cannot be improved or "fixed." God's only solution to the "self-life" is the cross.

It's important to make this clear. For many of us, we have never progressed beyond knowing the cross as something that happened "for" us 2,000 years ago and not as something operating in us in the here and now! That is the crux of the problem! The cross was not only where Christ died for us but also where we died with Him. Death is God's only solution to the "self" dilemma. That means our independent "self-life" must cease to be the source from which we live.

Those in leadership in ICCC had a familiar saying to illustrate this point. They said, "It's hard for an egg to fly". In other words, the outer shell was the thing that provided protection to the little chick inside. It was what kept it safe and comfortable. However, there came a point in its development when it had to break free from the shell and move into an entirely unknown environment. It had to die to that which had been its source of security and comfort in order to learn how to soar and become all it was always intended to be. Freedom required that it break through its natural confines into an entirely different dimension!

Sadly, to my mind, this goes a long way to explain the mediocrity and weakness we see within Christendom today. As Christians, we know we can do nothing to save ourselves, nevertheless, having received "forgiveness" and the assurance of Heaven, many of us continue to live out our Christianity from this underlying independent "self"-resourced mindset operating from the same source as we did before we encountered the Lord. Many of us haven't known any better! Religion and legalism, in very subtle and insidious ways, have put the onus on "self" to do all we are told we need to do to please God and sustain our Christian life. Paul challenged the Galatians on this very point. He said *"Are you so foolish and so senseless and so silly? Having begun [your new life spiritually] with the [Holy] Spirit, are you now reaching perfection [by dependence] on the flesh?"* (Gal 3:3 AMPC). One is "to walk in the flesh" the other is "walking in the Spirit".

That being the case, the vital question that we as Christians must ask ourselves is, "How do we break free from the limitations of the eggshell within which we were born and move beyond the confines of what is possible within the "self-life" and learn to soar into a life energised, resourced and sustained by the overcoming limitless life of the indwelling Christ, through the Holy Spirit?"

Chapter 10

The End of "Self"

To continue with my story, I was excited going into work the following Monday and was looking forward to what God was going to do. I had an inner sense of rest and peace as I no longer felt the burden to make things happen was mine to carry. Now, with God at the helm, I was sure success was guaranteed. Obviously, I still had to do all the practical things which needed to be done. The "rest" I was experiencing was not a rest of inactivity where I could act irresponsibly and with a lack of professionalism. It was a "heart rest" which had broken my dependence on the arm of the flesh to meet all the demands that life made off me. Therefore, everything still required my input and professional engagement across all the facets of managing the business. The difference was that I no longer relied on my input and effort but was looking to the Lord to provide for my needs.

I was in for a very big shock, however, because after a few weeks I realised that orders were not coming in as I had expected. In fact, they were not coming in at all. As time progressed and still no orders materialised I began to get seriously concerned. How could this happen? Did God not understand my need? Had I not placed my working life and the business into His hands along with everything else?

This brought back to me how vulnerable I had felt that Sunday morning at the conference in Northampton. Handing over control had made me feel like I was jumping off a high cliff without a safety harness. By giving up control I was, in effect, putting myself in a realm where my efforts could no longer dictate the outcome. I was now in free fall—utterly helpless! He had taken me at my word and He was now in control. There was nothing I could do to change or influence my situation.

This went on for a long and arduous 18 months! During this time we didn't sell one single machine. Not one! This was unprecedented! Never before, even in the deepest economic recessions had anything like this happened. Even all the regular "bread and butter" machines we sold on a frequent basis inexplicably stopped selling, and it seemed like everything we did ended in failure. We lost orders hand over fist.

The only thing that kept the company going was the Spare Parts and After Sales side of the business. As a company we were in bad shape. I remember being urgently summoned to a board meeting with the shareholders in our Dublin office. That was not a comfortable meeting. They asked me what my strategy was for recovery but I had nothing to say. I wasn't about to make vague statements or promises that sounded like I had it all under control. I felt inside that somehow it would all work out, but how could I explain to these guys what was really going on when I didn't quite understand myself?

Our financial year was from 1st October to end of September. Eighteen months had now passed since the March conference, and I didn't have a clue what was happening or why our order intake had just ground to an abrupt halt. It felt like we had hit an invisible brick wall!

Towards the end of that disastrous financial year, around mid-September, I received a call from a customer I knew quite well and had done business with before. He asked me to come and see him as he was looking to buy more machines. I made an appointment for that same afternoon and put the phone down but as I did, I was overcome with the pointlessness of even wasting the petrol going to visit him. I, and we as a company, had lost every order we had been involved in for the past 18 months so what was the point in driving 50 miles to talk with him?

On my way to the meeting I pondered these things and remember feeling confused and dejected about the situation. My thoughts were interrupted by what I realised was the Lord prompting me to pull the car over to the side of the road so that He could speak with me. This was most unusual!

As soon as I could, I came off the motorway and pulled the car over into a lay-by. Looking within and sensing His presence I recovered my peace and equilibrium. The Lord then began to speak to me. He assured me of His love and reminded me of what He had said at the conference. He told me that I was the *"apple of His eye"* and that as such He would respond with the same speed and protective instinct that we do when anything touches our eyes. He was my protector and I had nothing to fear. Then He went on to say that I should stop trying to "sell" my products and stop trying to persuade my customers to buy from me. He wanted me to simply trust Him as He would turn their hearts toward me and my products. I was to give good, honest, technical reasons for why they should select my products but not engage in all the usual "arm-twisting" sales techniques.

This brought an entirely new dimension to my thinking. This meant God would be at work in each and every enquiry we received, and I could depend on Him to turn those customers' hearts towards me and my products as He determined. This was a great relief to me as it no longer depended on me to do the whole "sales thing."

After a while I drove on to meet my customer. To my amazement he gave me an order of approximately £70,000, a decent order by 1993 standards. I was elated!

On my way home and feeling encouraged I decided to call in, on spec, with another customer. He promised me an order for around £120,000! This was just incredible! It was turning into quite a day but I was on a roll so I called in to see a third customer and secured yet another order for approximately £80,000. In truth this was an exceptional level of unexpected sales to secure in one day even in the best of times.

Our new financial year started some days later on the 1st of October and by the time we closed for the Christmas holidays the Lord had dropped into my lap orders with sufficient profit to pay the costs for the entire overhead of the company for the full financial year. Anything else we sold in the following nine months would be pure profit. This had nothing to do with me. I had done nothing differently to what I had previously; this was all God. Interestingly, this pattern continued for quite a number of years afterwards. October to December quarters produced sufficient profit to cover our overheads for the entire financial year even though up to that point our business had not been cyclical.

It was all a bit surreal to experience sales dropping into my lap in this way. Naturally, I often wondered why things turned out the way they did over this 18-month period and why it was necessary for me to go through that difficult time. As I look back at this now, I can see that there seemed to be two things the Lord was doing.

The first was leading me through the portal where the basis from which I lived my life would now be fundamentally altered. It moved from being characterised by striving and effort to being characterised by rest and reliance. This was a massive shift for me. It was the start of faith and dependence as a lifestyle, where He would settle me into a deep level of trust and reliance on Him alone in all the various areas of my life.

It was towards the end of this 18-month drought period that a single sentence started to come to me over and over again, especially when I was anxious and panicking at how badly things were going. I had never heard it before and wasn't at all sure from where it came. One evening it came to me so strongly I decided to see if it was in the Bible so I looked up a concordance and found it in Isaiah 7:9 NIV. This is the part of the verse which kept coming to me, *"If you do not stand firm in your faith, you will not stand at all."* Isn't that amazing! How gracious of the Lord to gently encourage me to maintain my dependent stance in the midst of apparent disaster. So this was to be my new "modus operandi." Standing was no longer the result of my striving and effort but the by-product of reliance and trust on the competence of another. Andrew Murray described this principle by saying, *"It is weakness entrusting itself to a mighty one to be kept, allowing itself to be upheld by omnipotent strength!"[11]*

The second equally significant thing He was doing was, although I had come to an end of reliance on what I could produce by my own efforts, the Lord needed to completely disabuse me from any lingering confidence in "self." "Self" can surely accomplish a great deal here in this visible, tangible dimension; however, it can accomplish nothing of eternal consequence. "Self" cannot "give birth to Spirit" (John 3:6 NIV). The problem with this is that the physical dimension is temporal, therefore what "flesh" or "self" gives birth to here in this physical dimension will pass away (fade and disappear). *"For all flesh is as grass, and all the glory of man as the flower of grass. The grass withereth, and the flower thereof falleth away"* (1 Peter 1:24). This is a law that we cannot circumvent!

To be clear, I'm talking about God bringing us to a place where we see that relying on "self" is like relying on a broken stick, and we simply are no longer able to trust it. Our confidence in it has been extinguished. Paul expressed this very clearly by saying, *"For it is we who are the circumcision, we who serve God by His Spirit, who boast in Christ Jesus, and who put no confidence in the flesh"* (Philippians 3:3 NIV). We now live from a different source (i.e., dependence on Christ within who is the Spirit). Those painful 18 months were God's way of functionally bringing me to this place where I inwardly realised the futility of my own efforts from God's perspective. He was cutting away my dependence on my own self-reliant, self-resourced "self."

---

11 Taken from Abide in Christ by Andrew Murray, chapter three, "Trusting Him to Keep you"

Cain's offering was rejected because he offered up to God the results he achieved by *"the sweat of his brow"* out of his own resources, which in God's eyes is under a curse and so can never be acceptable. The Scriptures are full of examples which testify to this truth! Abraham had to wait for Isaac until Sarah was past the point where she could naturally have children, Jacob was left with a limp after his encounter with God, Moses spent 40 years in the desert before he was ready to be used by God, Peter and Paul were brought to that same place where their dependence on "self" was broken before they could be used by God.

Jesus is the supreme example of someone who never operated from "self." He said, *"I am able to do nothing from Myself, independently, of My own accord"* (John 5:30 AMPC). If the Son was able to do nothing out of His "self," what makes us think that we are able to do what He could not? This "self-resourced," "self-sufficient," "self-reliant" thinking is part of the blindness that has infected humanity from the fall. This is the bridge we must all cross if we are to come into the abundant life. This is to open the door where functionally we live *"Not by might nor by power but by my Spirit says the Lord."*

Little did I know this was the truth the Lord was pointing me to that day at Spring Harvest nine years previously. God's word to me then from Psalm 18, where He promised to teach me how I could live *"beyond the level of my own ability,"* required that I first discover the utter futility of my own resources and efforts. God had to bring me to the end of myself, to the end of all my striving to succeed in life. Even my sincerest attempts to serve Him and to be pleasing to Him all had to end. God knows how to instruct us, and He very patiently and gently but very thoroughly, brings us to that point of death and resignation where we burn our bridges and never want to go back to those self-generating, self-reliant ways of living. This is where all our "self" delusions are stripped away and we fall helplessly headlong into Christ within as our only sufficiency and supply!

This is how the vital exchange takes place, the "self-life" steps down from its self-resourced, self-reliant management role and is replaced by the presence of the indwelling Christ who now assumes governance and control within. Life is very different from this point onwards!

Chapter 11

The Eye of the Needle

Many of us have been baptised as an outward symbolic statement that we have been "crucified with Christ," that we have "died" and been buried with Him. However, it is not enough to be baptised and hold an intellectual understanding of its symbolism. A "virtual death" is meaningless! God does not deal in virtual reality; there must be an "actual death" if we are to experience an "actual resurrection" into a new life. Before we install a new operating system, we must uninstall the old in actuality, not theory.

I believe this is why Paul, speaking to Christians in 2 Timothy 2:11 said, *"This is a faithful and trustworthy saying: If we died with Him, we will also live with Him;"* and again in Romans, *"Now if we be dead with Christ, we believe that we shall also live with Him"* (Romans 6:8). These verses have a primary particle of conditionality—'if'—in front of the statement. In other words, the second part of the sentence is conditional on the first being complied with. Paul is here highlighting the difference between the objective truth that "self" was crucified with Christ and the necessity for that to be subjectively outworked in our hearts. Paul is saying for us to "live" with Christ and know His presence within, we must first "die" with Him. According to these verses, the "death" of "self" is the central precondition that brings us into the functional efficacy of His life and the inner awareness of His wonderful presence in our everyday lives. This is not a symbolic death; it needs to be subjectively outworked in our experience.

That begs the critical question, What does it look like in our everyday lives when we say our "self" has been *"crucified with Christ"* and that we *have "died with Him"*? Clearly, this death does not mean that we cease to exist; otherwise, the whole discussion is meaningless. Neither is there any question of any part of us actually physically dying; that would be absurd. We remain fully human and active in all the various attributes of our humanity, our minds, our wills, and our bodies fully engaged in living life. Death in Scripture does not carry the thought of something ceasing to exist. Rather, the key thought is one of "separation." Indeed, Paul chose an Old Covenant term as an analogy which involved cutting away the flesh at the most sensitive part of the male anatomy used for procreation. He described this "subjective death" as "circumcision" (see Colossians 2:11).

So what does it mean to be "circumcised"? It's clear that Paul was not speaking about a physical circumcision since he said *"... and [true] circumcision is of the heart, a spiritual and not a literal [matter]"* (Romans 2:29 AMPC). This "circumcision" is the process whereby the objective truth that we were *"crucified with Christ,"* that we were *"baptised into His death"* becomes effective in our experience. Only when this objective truth becomes our own internal subjective reality can it be outworked in our lives.

Those verses in Ephesians 4 which instruct us to put off the "old self" (verse 22) and put on our "new self" (verse 24) are linked by verse 23 which gives us a vital clue into what this change actually is. It calls us to *"be renewed in the spirit of your mind"* (Ephesians 4:23). This "circumcision" is a profound, spiritual transformation in our hearts, understanding, and disposition. It is the process which removes the satanic-inspired deception that Adam came under in the garden. It is the divine surgeon cutting away our reliance on that false autonomous, self-resourced, self-reliant, "Self" which has dominated each of us from birth.

This truth was clearly outworked in Paul's own life. There was a time in his life, after his first encounter with the Lord on the road to Damascus, where this objective truth became a subjective reality in his own life. He describes his journey in Romans 7, but then in verse 11 he says, *"For sin, seizing an opportunity through the commandment, deceived me and through it killed me"* (Romans 7:11 ESV). He is telling us that his best attempts to keep the law and do the right thing, trying to please God out of his own ability and effort, brought Paul to the place where it *"killed him."* Law will do that to you! It was designed to do just that! This is when Paul came to an end of himself and died. He discovered "self's" complete inability to do anything that would be acceptable to God. Bishop H.C.G. Moule, talking about this transition in Paul's life, made this remarkable statement: *"(Paul) describes himself as passing from a state of soul in which, practically, his hope and strength was in himself, in which he lived and moved on the centre and in the atmosphere of self, to a state in which he was in Christ."*[12]

This is the process where "self" is unmasked as a counterfeit source. We now see it for what it is, a subtle but very hostile and virulent rival to the life of God and the activity of the Holy Spirit in our lives. Indeed, it is our enemy's ally within. We now realise "self" can only ever be rooted in fixed opposition to Christ's activity, operation, and purpose in our lives. In fact, this is the one essential differentiator between mere religion and authentic Christianity!

In effect, "circumcision" is where our dependence on "Self" is broken and we come into God's rest as we have already discussed at length. The "rest" we experience is because we are no longer relaying on our own resources and our own efforts. We have "died" to anything within ourselves, either as a means for pleasing God or, since there is no spiritual or secular divide, for living every other aspect of our lives.

---

12 Taken from Bishop H.C.G. Moule's little book "Thoughts on Union with Christ," pg 20. He was the Bishop of Durham, principal of Ridley Hall, Cambridge, and Honorary Chaplain to Queen Victoria, a leading theologian and author in the later part of the nineteenth and early twentieth century.

This effectively ties our hands as we discover that we have no other source from which we can draw the resources necessary to live our lives. It is this realisation that throws us entirely on Christ. We then effectively *"cease from our own works"* and *"enter God's rest"* (Hebrews 4). That is when we find our centre of gravity moves out of "self" into Christ Himself within. This is the context for what Jesus said, *"Blessed are the poor in spirit: for theirs is the Kingdom of Heaven"* (Matthew 5:3).

Colossians 2:11 NIV is one of those definitive verses on this topic. *"In Him you were also circumcised with a circumcision not performed by human hands. Your whole "self" ruled by the flesh was put off when you were circumcised by Christ."* It is when *"our whole self ruled by the flesh"* is replaced by *"our whole self ruled by the Spirit"* that everything changes, and the floodgates of the fullness of Christ fills our lives. This is the necessary process where the caterpillar turns into a butterfly! *"Let us therefore fear, lest, a promise being left us of entering into His rest, any of you should seem to come short of it"* (Hebrews 4:1).

There is no possibility of change for those who have not reversed the decision made by our father Adam. Critically, we must each choose to go back to functionally living from "rest" as Adam did originally. His first full day in the garden was the seventh day, the day of rest, and he continued to live from rest in a dependent, God-centred, God-resourced posture until that tragic day he chose to opt out of it.

The Lord knows how to bring us to the end of "Self's" resources. How He brings that about will be different for each of us. It may be through circumstances or simply by revelation and the conviction of the Holy Spirit. As I have already shared, in my case He took me through 18 months of a severe drought in my working life and then turned the whole situation around in one day. Whatever way He chooses, He prepares us so that we voluntarily permit Him to cut away our reliance on our "self-resourced" capability. The greater our own tenacity and perceived resources, the greater the pressure He may bring to bear in order to get us to that place where "self" realises its own limitations and gladly and willingly runs into the provision and resources that are Christ.

This is how we exit the "Self-life" and functionally exchange it for "His life" (Colossians 3:4). It opens the door for us to say with Paul, *"I am crucified with Christ: nevertheless I live; yet not I, but Christ liveth in me"* (Galatians 2:20). He then lives His life through us, lifting us above the level of what we can produce by our own striving and efforts.

I have shared how this became real to me and what a relief and blessing it is to be free from all the pressure of trying to get it right and conduct myself in the way I thought I should. The harder I tried, the deeper I sank. Then, that day at the conference in Northampton, I simply could not keep on doing it and I ground to a halt. I came to an end of myself. I stopped all my striving which was when the "Spirit" was then able to take over. The joy and freedom has not stopped flowing since. What a weight rolls off our shoulders as we discover that Christ is our total answer and all-inclusive source for everything!

Major Ian Thomas describes how he found his breakthrough in this area: *"Then, one night in November, that year, just at midnight, I got down on my knees before God, and I just wept in sheer despair. I said, 'With all my heart I have wanted to serve Thee. I have tried to my uttermost and I am a hopeless failure.' That night things happened. The Lord seemed to make plain to me that night, through my tears of bitterness: 'You see, for seven years, with utmost sincerity, you have been trying to live for Me, on My behalf, the life that I have been waiting for seven years to live through you.' Thomas later reflected: 'I got up the next morning to an entirely different Christian life, but I want to emphasise this: I had not received one iota more than I already had for seven years!'"*[13]

---

13 From Major Ian Thomas's book The Saving Life of Christ, Zondervan

Let me just say, for most of us, this is the culmination of what can be a lengthy process. Often, we have to learn by our constant failure, by discovering that all our best endeavours, our will power, our spiritual disciplines are simply inadequate. As a result, our disillusionment and frustration grows until something finally snaps within us. We simply cannot continue and we give up all hope that we, by our own efforts, can ever live this life. This is where "self" subjectively dies! Again, that's not to say it will never raise its ugly head again as it will remain a constant threat to us. However, it is at this point that something fundamental changes within us and, from then onwards, we walk with a limp so to speak. Andrew Murray put it this way, *"A believer may know that he is free and yet have to admit that his experience is that of a hopeless captive. ... It is in the utter despair of self that entire surrender to the Spirit is born and strengthened. Ceasing from all hope through the flesh and the law is entrance into the liberty of the Spirit."*[14]

Jesus emphasised this truth by saying, *"If any man will come after me, let him deny himself"* (Matthew 16:24). Jesus is not here calling for "Self" to deny itself. He is not saying that "Self" should marshall all its resources in a vain attempt to stop being or doing what "Self" is or does and by suppressing "Self's" natural impulses. No indeed! He is saying we must deny "Self," side-stepping it entirely as the means and resource from which we live, choosing instead to step into *"Christ who is our life"* (Colossians 3:4). To use "Self" to deny "Self," which is, in effect, the common understanding, is mere religion, a swim in a swamp and a recipe for abject misery and defeat.

It is *"the Spirit who gives life; the flesh COUNTS FOR NOTHING"* (John 6:63 NIV—capitals mine). Paul left us in no doubt when he said, *"Now this I say, brethren, that flesh and blood cannot inherit the Kingdom of God"* (1 Corinthians 15:50). This hard truth is further confirmed in Galatians: *"For he that soweth to his flesh shall of the flesh reap corruption; but he that soweth to the Spirit shall of the Spirit reap life everlasting"* (Galatians

---

14 Andrew Murray, from his book The Indwelling Spirit, chapter 18

6:8-9). The biblical understanding of "sowing" refers to the means or the vehicle we are using in order to achieve or produce an intended outcome. The seed we sow determines the harvest we get. If we are using "self" as our seed, as the source we depend on to live our lives, we will reap only one result—corruption. Then the Book of Romans removes any lingering doubt on this subject. *"So then they that are in the flesh cannot please God"* (Romans 8:8). Notice the term used: "in the flesh" (i.e., operating out of an independent mindset relying on our natural resources and abilities as our source for living life). That applies irrespective of how good or noble our actions appear on the surface. It is only when what Paul said becomes true of us personally that we will have come to the end of "Self." *"For it is we who are the circumcision, we who serve God by His Spirit, who boast in Christ Jesus, and who put no confidence in the flesh* (Philippians 3:3). That succinctly describes this most liberating experience. Here, we are confronted with the irrefutable reality of what Jesus said, *"Apart from Me, cut off from vital union with Me you can do nothing"* (John 15:5 AMPC).

Jesus then used a different analogy in the Gospel of Mark: *"Children, how hard it is to enter the Kingdom of God! It is easier for a camel to go through the eye of a needle than for someone who is rich to enter the Kingdom of God"* (Mark 10:24-25 NIV). Although the context is about money we know money in and of itself is not the problem. It's our attitude to it that needs to be corrected. The problem is that we use it to authenticate that sense of autonomous self-sufficiency and self-competence with which we have all been infected.

All the Alpha male characteristics so valued and promoted in our society are a demonstration of "self's" activity under satan's operation. It is an expression of the same spirit that prompted the building of the Tower of Babel which God immediately rejected and judged. Unfortunately, this spirit is also evident in many Christian institutions and, sadly, too often in those in Christian leadership. There is little or no understanding within the body of Christ that this all flows from a satanic-inspired source. It is simply "self" manifesting its master's trademark!

This then is the context, not just for describing what our "Self" or "old Self" looks like but also for explaining why it is so critical that we functionally "put it off" as Ephesians 4:22-24 instructs us. As we yield up control and receive this truth by faith, the Holy Spirit can then start to change this dynamic so that Christ becomes our life.

To summarise, we can live out of dependence on who and what we are "in Christ" or we can live depending on "self" and what it can produce. That is the stark choice! As already indicated, in Scripture one is called *"walking in the Spirit"*; the other is *"walking in the flesh"* (Galatians 5:16). These are mutually exclusive alternatives!

Chapter 12
The "New Self" – Union

We have identified what the "Self-life" looks like in a functional way. We have also described how we put it off and uninstall the enemy's rogue operating system so to speak. Now we need to understand how the manufacturer's new "operating system" is installed and how we "put on" our "new self" functionally. An understanding of how this "new self" becomes a reality in us opens the door for us to experience the positive, dynamic flow of the very life of Christ continually bubbling up within us. This is where we take on our new identity!

It wasn't until I understood this next amazing piece of the jigsaw that I was able to grasp how I became a "new self." Without wanting to overstate it, this is where we start to experience wholeness and an increasing sense of completeness. Many need to go from where they know they are forgiven and certain of Heaven and move on into the enjoyment of a life lived from rest in the fullest expression of their "new identity" "in Christ." The Lord lovingly wants to draw us, like a moth to the flame, into this most intimate, real, inner awareness of Himself. The truth we are now considering cannot fail to sweep away every sense of deficiency, defeat and lack.

Sadly, the reality for many of us has been that for too long we have lived from a self-identity essentially the same as before we came to the Lord. Our identity has not changed. We still see ourselves as sinners, albeit now forgiven sinners, so we effectively operate out of the same old reality we lived from before. In effect, our internal reality has never caught up with our new spiritual reality of being a "new self." If all we know in our hearts is forgiveness, that alone will not empower us to live any differently to how we once did. A complete salvation must not only deal with the penalty of sin but must deliver us from the power of it as well.

My experience is that to live the Christian life without experiencing the reality of being a "new self" is to live in mediocrity and spiritual poverty. We could equate it to a caterpillar that never transitioned to a butterfly. If that is to change, we must understand how we "put on" the "new self" (Ephesians 4:24). Only the "new self" identity "in Christ" can live *"like God in true righteousness and holiness"* (Ephesians 4:24 NIV). In other words, this "new self" expresses itself in *"true righteousness and holiness"* as an unforced natural outflow. The "new self" does not live in defeat and failure any more than Christ could.

The Scripture in 2 Corinthians expresses in unmistakable terms the massive difference living from this "new self" identity makes. *"Therefore if any man be in Christ, he is a new creature: old things are passed away; behold, all things are become new"* (2 Corinthians 5:17). Two things we need to notice in that verse. One is that it speaks of a change of identity. We actually become a new creature or a "new species of being." We are no longer who we once were. Secondly, the words "all things" tell us that everything, without exception, is now different from our previous life.

The various stages that bring about this "new self" are described in Ephesians 2:4-6. It says, *"But God, who is rich in mercy, for His great love wherewith He loved us, even when we were dead in sins, hath quickened us together with Christ, and hath raised us up together, and made us sit together in heavenly places in Christ Jesus."*

The three uses of the word "together" in that verse define this next stage.

1   Our "Self" has been "quickened together with Christ."
2   Our "Self" has been "raised up together with Christ."
3   Our "Self" has been "made to sit together in heavenly places in Christ."

This verse takes us from the "death" side of the cross and brings us to the "resurrection" side of the cross. We see that the very same "self" that died, as we discussed in the previous chapters, is now "quickened," "raised up," and is now "seated in heavenly places in Christ." "Self" is now "together" with Christ and settled into this new "in Christ" reality, in a new dynamic and a new identity. "Self," no longer acting in independence, is now wholly dependent, energized, and empowered through a new and living connection with the resurrected Christ.

However, it is in understanding the essential nature of this connection that we now have with Christ that we uncover a vital key. This discovery unlocks our 'new self' identity in Christ.

Scripture uses various expressions to describe this "connection," but there is a common denominator which underpins them all. The verse that best describes the essential nature of our "together" connection with Christ is 1 Corinthians 6:17: *"But the one who is united and joined to the Lord is one spirit with Him"* (AMPC). Here, we discover the exact nature of this vital connection we now enjoy with the Lord. It is described as being "joined to the Lord" so we become "one spirit" with Him. As such we must interpret all other biblical descriptions of our proximity or "together" connection to Christ through the lens that we have been *"joined to Christ"* to the point of becoming *"one spirit with Him."*

This is saying that we are united to the Lord because His Spirit and our spirit have become "one Spirit." This is immense! God is spirit[15] yet our

---

15 John 4:24

spirit becomes one spirit with His Spirit. It is not that He has come to dwell within us as if we were side by side in close proximity, as a visitor in our home who uses the guest bedroom. It is not simply that we are "positionally" together with Him in some theological, conceptional way. No, it goes much deeper. Colossians 3 states it this way: *"For you died, and your life is now hidden with Christ in God. When Christ, who is your life ..."* (Colossians 3:3-4 NIV). That word "with" in the original is *"syn"* which, according to Strong's definition is "a primary preposition denoting union with or together."[16] The original Greek is saying our life is now *"hidden in union with Christ"* to the point that HE becomes our life. This is a vital union where our human spirit becomes "one Spirit" with the divine Spirit. This fundamentally changes what "self" used to be. This is the birth of a "new self."

So, we find ourselves in Romans 6:5, *"one with Him"*, Christ and you now "one spirit"! Having given all of ourselves unreservedly over to Him and He, having given all of Himself unreservedly to us, we now enter into a dynamic union, a new relation one to the other. This "union" connection we now enjoy with Christ is the conduit through which the transformational capacity for change comes. This is the point where the dam in the river bursts wide open allowing the abundant river of life to flow without restriction and without limitation. As our eyes are opened to what our "new self" actually is and we grasp the incredible reality of our union with the resurrected Christ, the dynamic valve is opened within us to the enjoyment of all that belongs to us "in Christ."

In order to give full expression to the extent and nature of this "union" connection, the language we must use may imply more than is intended. So, in advance, we need to draw a line of demarcation here and clearly state that in this union we humans remain fully human. There is no implication that we become divine. Having said that though, we now find ourselves in a milk in coffee, sugar in tea, sand and cement type of union, but the milk never becomes coffee or the tea sugar, nor does sand

---

16 From "The Exhaustive Concordance of the Bible" generally knows as Strong's Concordance.

become cement. Indeed, the ingredients together become something entirely different to what they otherwise are on their own. We now find ourselves irretrievably joined into one entity with the divine. All distinctions blending together as one spirit, yet without losing any of each party's uniqueness and distinctiveness, without any loss of each party's personality and individuality, without any loss of our unique self-conscious identity.

So let us state this in all its enormity. We are fully united with divinity, spirit joined with Spirit creating one new entity, a new humanity, a new species of being—something we never were before and a race of humans that never existed before. We are united in such a close and intimate way that removes all separation from our divine source. Indeed, our spirit plus Christ's Spirit becomes one Spirit, not two. Dan Stone put it mathematically to great effect, *"one plus one equals one (1+1=1), the divine and the human have become one."*[17] We are spirit beings who express ourselves through our souls and our bodies. Now, though, our spirit has become one with Christ's Spirit transforming who we really are! We are now united, made one with our divine source.

This, to our natural mind, is a paradox! Nevertheless, the rebirth of "self" happens as a direct result of our spirit becoming one with Christ's Spirit. Indeed, it is because we have become "one spirit" in union with Him that we are "resurrected," "quickened together," and "seated with Him in heavenly places." A real, vital, dynamic union has taken place. We are now indivisibly united to Christ in all His attributes and competences. We have moved from being dead, that is, separated from Him, to being alive in union with Him. We have become one with the source of "life" Himself. We no longer see ourselves as independent, separated, forgiven sinners seeking to get closer to Him. Instead, we settle into the abiding, unchanging reality that together we are "one spirit." We cannot get any closer than that!

---

17 Dan Stone, author, pastor and Bible teacher, wrote this wonderful book *The Rest of the Gospel—When the partial gospel has worn you out!* This is an extract from that book.

The illusion of our independence and separation from our divine source can now be finally unmasked. Christ can now become our unchanging daily experience because "He is our life." Who and what we are have changed! This new internal connection we have with Christ transports us into a completely new realm to the one we once had. This is so much more than forgiveness for all of our past misdeeds, wonderful as that is. This unites us with the unending transformative flow of divine life. This transforming Presence is now united with us and to us and is now living through us!

Indeed, this truth explains how Ephesians 1 can become ours functionally: "... *who hath blessed us with all spiritual blessings in heavenly places in Christ*" (Ephesians 1:3). We should notice where these "*spiritual blessings*" are located. They are in this other dimension of reality, here called "heavenly places." That's not here in this physical dimension. As a young Christian I could only mentally accept these statements as true because they were in Scripture, but these blessings all seemed to be one step removed from me in this other faraway, unseen realm. I could never figure out how I could experience them in the here and now where I needed them most. This was the boundary line between what was functional and what was only a mental concept.

Intellectually, I knew that I had been placed "in Christ" but functionally it had no real practical outworking. It was just abstract information. I also knew that Christ had taken up residence within me when I was born again but back then I had very little inner awareness of that fact. To me these were two separate truths with no correlation one to the other. It was only when the reality of union with Christ dawned that everything fell into place. I saw that Christ is the common denominator between these two dimensions. A flash of realisation bridged the gap as the Holy Spirit brought them together. I realised that union with Christ is the central core reality. So when Scripture talks about "Christ in us," it is speaking about our union with Christ from earth's perspective. When Scripture talks about us being "in Christ" it is speaking about our union with Christ from Heaven's perspective. Union is the central underpinning reality that makes both these facets vital and real. They are, in fact, flip sides of the same coin! It is because "Christ is in us" that we are "in Christ," and both of these realities are brought about as a result of our indissoluble union to Christ! We see this stated in 1 John 4:13: *"By this we know, with confident assurance that we abide in Him and He in us, because He has given to us His Holy Spirit"* (AMPC). It is because the Holy Spirit has come into union with our spirit that we become *"one spirit"* (1 Corinthians 6:17 AMPC). That, in turn, ushers us into the functional experience that *"we abide in Him and He in us."*

In other words, although we live in this physical realm, the fact that "Christ is in us" permanently connects us to *"all spiritual blessings in heavenly places in Christ"* (Ephesians 1:3), thus making them our own. "Christ in us" has not just opened up the way, but He Himself becomes the way we can enjoy all these awesome "spiritual blessings" in a functional way. That has enormous implications and is a vital key to grasp!

Primary among all these "spiritual blessings" that now belong to us is the fact that through our union with HIM we have direct access into the immediate presence of the Father. *"For through him we both have access to the Father by one Spirit"* (Ephesians 2:18 NIV). We know the veil in the temple in Jerusalem was torn from top to bottom when Jesus died. This was not just a symbolic gesture; it was the external manifestation of a brand new spiritual reality. It was declaring that every obstacle and everything that had separated God from His man ever since Eden's Garden had now been removed. Unrestricted access into the immediate and vital, dynamic presence of God was now freely available for all to enjoy. Not in theory nor as a mere intellectual concept but real, conscious, vital access into His immediate presence. Access without qualification, without compliance to an external code of conduct, without having to earn it, now available to each and every human.

Whoever now wishes to enter into this hallowed place where the tangible, conscious presence of God resides can now approach freely through the "new and living way" that has been opened up. That way is Christ Himself! This holy presence, however, no longer resident in a building in Jerusalem or any other modern-day building for that matter (Acts 7:48) but now resident within everyone who has been born of the Spirit. This, for the very first time, allows broken, fallen humanity free, unrestricted access into the "Holy of Holies" to enjoy real spirit-to-Spirit contact. There, we fellowship with the Father and the Son in a deep Spirit-to-spirit intimacy of "knowing Him" within us. This is what Hebrews is saying: *"Having therefore, brethren, boldness to enter into the holiest by the blood of Jesus, By a new and living way, which He hath consecrated for us, through the veil ... Let us draw near with a true heart in full assurance of faith"* (Hebrews 10:19-22).

This, of course, brings everything together in a wonderful harmony. Our union with Christ brings these two aspects of truth into convergence. "Christ in us" unites us to all that we are "in Christ." It unites us to all He is in Himself, not "positionally" as a theological concept but functionally. It brings all that is ours in "heavenly places" down to the cut and thrust of our everyday life. We are now joined, through our union with Christ, to all the resources of the Godhead. This is how Paul was able to say, "Ye are complete in *him*" (Colossians 2:10). John said, *"In this [union and communion with Him] love is brought to completion and attains perfection with us ... because as He is, so are we in this world"* (1 John 4:17 AMPC). If that statement doesn't make us stop and think, we haven't understood it! As He is complete, *"so are we in this world."* Indeed, we are complete with His completeness. The prodigal's father said it this way: "Son, you are always with me, and all that is mine is yours" (Luke 15:31 AMPC).

If we can grasp this, it will remove every consciousness of lack, deficiency, and weakness. It will remove the familiar debilitating sense of guilt and failure. It will remove the deep-seated orphaned mindset so deeply ingrained in our psyche. It changes forever who and what we are. It empowers radical change since everything is now restored to us "in Christ" in us! All our brokenness, our orphaned identity, every trace of the fall is now in effect united to an omnipotent, glorious, divine rescuer within. Everything is now found "in Him" in us. Victory is now a person *"seated in heavenly places"* within us, united to us, living His overcoming, abundant, victorious life through us! This is a wonderful, awe-inspiring truth from which to live our lives! This is our "new self"!

Chapter 13

The Awareness of the Indwelling Presence

A Christianity without the inward witness of Christ is an inferior version of what the Father has provided for His children. Even under the Old Covenant it is clear that God's Presence played a vital role in the lives of the Israelites and was an integral part of their experience and understanding. His Presence was real and visible day and night during the wilderness years! It was not something you could be in any doubt about. His Presence was experienced at the tent of meeting. He also resided in the tabernacle and in both temples above the Mercy Seat sitting over the Ark of the Covenant in the Holy of Holies.

A.W. Tozer said, *"Ransomed men need no longer pause in fear to enter the Holy of Holies. God wills that we should push on into His presence and live our whole life there. This is to be known in conscious experience. It is more than a doctrine—to be held; it is a life to be enjoyed every moment of every day."* He then went on, *"The world is perishing for lack of the knowledge of God, and the church is famishing for want of His presence."*[18]

The doorway into this experience is not clearly defined or perhaps even understood today. There seems to be little emphasis and value placed on it, yet we all live our everyday lives from "internal consciousness." That's just the way we function so the only question is what or who is going to fill our "internal consciousness." If not the presence of Christ, then what?

---

18 A.W. Tozer's book The Pursuit of God, chapter "Removing the Veil," pg. 36 & 38

That makes what James M. Campbell said highly pertinent. He said, *"The work of Christ in its entireness must be brought within the inner sphere of personal consciousness; the outward Christ of history must become the Christ of inward experience; the dead Christ of Calvary must become the living Christ of the present; the Christ embalmed in a book must dwell and reign within the heart. It is not Christ upon the cross, nor Christ within the Bible, nor Christ in heaven that saves; but Christ deeply hidden in the inmost spirit; Christ constantly present in the life; Christ the inspiration of every thought and word and deed. Christ in the soul and not Christ buried in a tomb."[19]*

The central promise of the New Covenant is that we can come to know the inner reality of this transforming presence in an up close and personal way. A.W. Pink said, *"The grand end of our vital, saving, and practical union with Christ is to bring us into experimental oneness with Him: that we may drink in His spirit, have His mind, share His joy. Of all the experiences of God's saints on earth this approximates nearest to the heavenly bliss. Experimental union consists of knowing, loving, enjoying Christ: it is having plain, practical, personal dealings with Him."[20]* That is pure, crystal clear water to a parched and thirsty soul!

A.W. Tozer said this, *"There is at the root of true religion an inward witness, an awareness of God and Christ at the farthest-in core of the renewed Christian's spirit given to him by the Spirit of God. ... It is the end result of Bible doctrine but it is not that doctrine. It is a consciousness of God and spiritual things too deep and wonderful to utter or even think."[21]*

The gift of the Holy Spirit can become a "felt" reality in us and to us. His Presence is recognisable, as is His absence. A "Christianity" without this inner dynamic of the Holy Spirit is no more than human effort wearing religious clothing.

---

19 A.W. Tozer's book The Pursuit of God, chapter "Removing the Veil," pg. 36 & 38
20 From A.W. Pink's book Spiritual Union and Communion under the chapter heading "Experimental Union"
21 Taken from A.W. Tozer's book The Dangers of a Shallow Faith: Awakening from Spiritual Lethargy.

Jesus promised that He would "manifest" Himself to those who loved Him in John 14:21. Paul commended the Corinthian Christians to the "fellowship of the Holy Spirit" and assumed this "inner-knowing" posture as the norm for Christians. He then confirmed that by telling them *"Since we live by the Spirit, let us keep in step with the Spirit"* (Galatians 5:25 NIV). How are we to do that if we don't recognise or know His presence? This is a subjective walk where we live by dependence on the Spirit and follow the Holy Spirit's leading within. It is not referring to an intellectual or cerebral walk where we seek to obey biblical principles and work out "Christian values." Indeed, the verse we saw previously in Revelation 3:20 defines, in emphatic and unmistakable terms, not just that Christ comes into us but that the place where we encounter Him and enjoy real intimacy and fellowship with Him is now within, not without. *"I will come in to him, and will sup with him, and he with me"* (Revelation 3:20). Romans 8 is quite explicit. *"The Spirit itself beareth witness with our spirit, that we are the children of God"* (Romans 8:16). This is saying that it is the norm for God's children to have this inner Spirit-to-spirit "witness."

Oddly, many Christians seem to place a greater emphasis on studying the Scriptures without an equal and corresponding emphasis on knowing the presence of the One to whom the entirety of Scripture points. Their "internal consciousness" of the indwelling presence is negated in favour of having an intellectual knowledge-based understanding of the Book. They would never say this but it's as if, for them, God is Father, Son, and Holy Scriptures. The immediacy of the Holy Spirit's presence has been relegated to a mere nominal, intellectual concept rather than a vital, internal, dynamic reality from which they live their lives. This is in direct and stark contrast to Paul's prayer for the Ephesians. He prayed *"[that you may come] to know [practically, through personal experience] the love of Christ which far surpasses [mere] knowledge ... that you may be filled up [throughout your being] to all the fullness of God [so that you may have the richest experience of God's presence in your lives, completely filled and flooded with God Himself]* (Ephesians 3:19 AMP). What could be more wonderful or more desirable?

It is too easy for us to value a mental and theological understanding of what the Book says, whilst at the same time, virtually ignoring the immediate presence of the Author Himself dwelling within. Important as Bible knowledge is, and it is vitally important, it can only ever point us to something beyond itself. The reality and substance to which it points is not found in a cerebral understanding of what it says.

Jesus exposed the critical distinction between the pursuit of biblical knowledge and the internal reality to which it points. He said, *"Ye search the Scriptures; for in them ye think ye have eternal life: and they are they which testify of me. And ye will not come to me, that ye might have life"* (John 5:39-40). That is a very subtle but vital distinction: It's one thing to know the Word of God and that is, of course, important, however, it is quite a different thing to intimately and inwardly know the God of the Word through the Holy Spirit!

A map can be of vital importance but only if used as it is intended. It is good to know the map but that is not the objective. Its true purpose is to lead us to our destination. Our destination is an inner, intimate, divine experience with a person, the reality of Christ Himself reigning within, made alive and real to us by the Holy Spirit. Paul was not behind the door in stating what he prioritised above absolutely everything else. He said, *"I count everything as loss compared to the possession of the priceless privilege [the overwhelming preciousness, the surpassing worth, and supreme advantage] of knowing Christ Jesus my Lord"* (Philippians 3:8 AMPC).

I'm not devaluing Scripture in the least, I'm elevating Christ as a living, dynamic agent made real in us by His Spirit. He alone is the bringer and implementor of His Kingdom in our lives. It is because He lives in us that we have His life. It is the awareness of our union with Christ and the enjoyment of His presence in us that changes everything!

The central point I'm making is that to live our lives out of "self," with our minds focussed on biblical knowledge of an external Jesus, who walked this earth 2,000 years ago, is to miss the power of the divine connection entirely. Why is that? Because *"the letter kills, but the Spirit gives life"* (2 Corinthians 3:6 NIV).

Miguel de Molinos, in the 17th century, prized and valued the overflowing reality of Christ dwelling within above everything else. He said, *"Enter into that inmost realm, for it's there you may overcome outward surroundings. Within you is a divine fortress, and that divine fortress defends, protects and fights for you. Observe, please, a man who has as his house a great fortress; that man is not upset though his enemies pursue him and surround him. He need only retreat into the great citadel. YOU have a strong castle (deep within you) that will make you triumphant over all enemies. Yes, those which are visible and those which are invisible. That castle dwells within you NOW, regardless of all snares and tribulations, IT IS THERE! Within it dwells the divine Comforter. Retreat there, for THERE all is quiet, peaceful, secure and calm."* He then goes on, *"Why seek the Lord by means of straining the brain, in searching for some place to go to pray, in selecting points to discuss, and in straining to find a God without ... when you have Him within you? We simply shall not find our God without. Nor shall we find Him by means of reasoning and logic and surface information. Each of us has Him present within us. There seems to be a blindness in those believers who always seek God, cry for Him, long for Him, invoke His name, pray to Him daily, while never discovering that they themselves are a living Temple and His one TRUE habitation. Their own spirit is the seat and throne of a God who continually rests within them."*[22]

We can say, therefore, to know Him is to know Him within. To state the obvious, to know the presence of Christ is to know Christ Himself as an up close and intimate reality. It is indeed this "knowing" that moves us from a cerebral or intellectual knowledge-based belief system into a vital, life-giving, life-transforming union reality. This is abiding in

---

22 Taken from Miguel de Molinos book The Spiritual Guide

the "Holy of Holies" within our own inner sanctuary. Andrew Murray made this distinction clear. He said, *"God is known not by understanding, but by the heart. Only love can know God in truth. The true nature of redemption is inward. A Christ not in us is the same as a Christ not ours. Death to self and Christ alive in us is the only salvation."*[23]

Indeed, the inner awareness of His presence becomes our confirmation that "He's got us" and that "we've got Him." 1 John 4:13 spells this out for us: *"By this we know, with confident assurance that we abide in Him and He in us, because He has given to us His Holy Spirit"* (AMPC). This is saying that we know we *"abide in Him"* and *"He in us"* because we have our own personal inner awareness of Christ by the Holy Spirit. This is again explicitly stated in 1 John 5:10: *"He who believes in the Son of God who adheres to, trusts in, and relies on Him has the testimony [possesses this divine attestation] within himself"* (AMPC).

These two statements take us out of the theological, mental understanding of these biblical truths into the experiential reality of them. It turns the external cerebral focus within much of Christendom on its head! This is a foundational, vital step-change to make.

Every born-again child of God is a container, an earthen vessel,[24] which carries the treasure of the fullness of the risen Christ. We are now carriers of His presence. The primary function and activity of a container is simply to hold something. A cup finds its purpose in what it contains, be that tea, coffee or whatever. It is a foundational part of our new identity to see ourselves, not just mentally but in our experience, as containers of the omnipotent, indwelling Christ every moment of the day, every day of the year.

Importantly, He doesn't come and go depending on how we have performed. Also, if we are born-again, it is impossible for us to get more

---

23 Quote from "Introduction" chapter of Andrew Murray's little book Wholly for God.
24 2 Corinthians 4:7

of Him. He came in the completeness of who He is to stay and make His home in us and unite Himself to us. Jesus promised that He would never leave us and that a river would spring up within every born-again Christian who drank of the water that He gave. This is speaking of Christ's very presence and activity within us through the Holy Spirit.

It's wonderful to know the divine Presence in our corporate gatherings although that may not happen as often as we would like. However, my point is that these occasions can never become a substitute for the personal, inner experience of union with that divine Presence. What we experience behind four walls in a safe and secure environment on a Sunday morning will not sustain us on Monday morning in the office or factory floor. We need our own ongoing, inner supply.

As I have shared, because my Christianity felt so feeble and the reality of His Presence within felt so shallow I used to think that I needed more of Him, not realising the truth was that He had already taken up residence within me in all His fullness. Let me be absolutely clear what the reason was for this feeble, debilitating, frustrating experience. The burning issue was not that I needed more of Him but that He needed more of me!

Like a ship sinking into the ocean, the supply of water will fill it and occupy all the available spaces except those already occupied. It is not the lack of water that prevents every last corner of the sinking vessel being filled; it is the fact that there are areas already occupied with other things. For many, although Christ has taken up residence within their containers, religion and legalism operating from a self-resourced mindset struggling and striving to do what we think God expects of us means they are still operating from the "self-life." This restricts His activity and presence within, blocking their internal awareness of Him. The power of the "self-life" has not yet been broken and is still very much in charge. Naturally, then, this is what fills their awareness. I cannot over-emphasise that this is what must change! This is the vital key that, once turned in the lock, allows the very real awareness of His nearness and intimate presence to flood our lives.

A.W. Tozer reinforces that this is where the blockage lies. He says, *"'Self' is the opaque veil that hides the face of God from us. It can be removed only in spiritual experience, never by mere instruction. We may as well try to instruct leprosy out of our system. There must be a work of God before we are free. We must invite the cross to do its deadly work within us."*[25]

Interestingly, in the Tabernacle and the Temple there was a golden table on which the shewbread was set. "Shewbread" literally means "bread of the face" or a more appropriate translation might be "bread of the Presence." The symbolism is unmistakable. God's Presence was to be the priests' daily bread! It was the thing that fed and sustained them. Jesus confirmed this in John 6:57 AMPC: *"Whoever continues to feed on Me [whoever takes Me for his food and is nourished by Me] shall [in his turn] live through and because of Me."* This is much more than reading our Bibles; it is feeding on HIM in a direct, immediate acquaintance with Him by the Holy Spirit within.

Most importantly, in closing this chapter, we should always remember that our consciousness of His Presence is a subjective variable, especially in the early days of our walk, whereas the reality of His Presence abiding in us is not. It is an objective, settled reality that does not fluctuate or change. Also, when we talk about our awareness of His Presence, we are not referring to "feelings" or the usual caricature of "goose bumps" or some other emotional or physical manifestation. All this is rooted in faith as our fixed posture. Having said that, faith must always produce the "substance" of what we have believed, so this gives us this inner witness (or confirmation) we are talking about. We saw this in 1 John: *"He who believes in the Son of God, who adheres to, trusts in, and relies on Him, has the testimony, possesses this divine attestation, within himself"* (1 John 5:10 AMPC).

---

25 From A.W. Tozer's book The Pursuit of God, chapter "Removing the Veil," pg 46.

This is the Shalom of God, the touchstone of His presence within, and there is so much more to this awareness than what we may initially grasp. A study of the word "shalom" makes clear that it encompasses everything we today would describe as wholeness, completeness, tranquility, to be made safe, fulfilled, blessed, victorious, healthy, and prosperous.

Chapter 14

A New Identity

Oswald Chambers made this insightful statement: *"Salvation is not merely deliverance from sin, nor the experience of personal holiness; the salvation of God is deliverance out of "self" entirely into union with Himself."*[26] It is as a result of our union with Christ that we become an entirely new entity compared to who we were before. Our spirit has become one with the divine! This fact changes everything. His Presence now residing within becomes the solid, unchanging reality from which we live and the cornerstone of our new identity. This is a place of adequacy and sufficiency, a place of complete rest.

We get up every morning and face the day with a spring in our step, knowing that everything is now different. We are no longer alone. Neither is life all down to us since we are forever united to Him in a fixed, unchanging connection. The "old self" has ceased all its striving and all its autonomous "Self" resourced operations. All that tortured self-reliance and the demands of living out of separation from our divine source are now exchanged for a life of perpetual union and rest. This lifts us up to a life where our ability is no longer the defining factor. Christ's Presence now floods our inner awareness as part of our self-identity.

That being the case we can legitimately express our union in the words coined by Norman Grubb: "Christ as us."[27] It is only as we express it

---

26 From Oswald Chambers' book My Utmost for His Highest, 13th March
27 This term was coined by Norman Grubb, sometimes personalised as "Christ as me." Used in several of his books such as No Independent Self, Zerubabel Press, pg. 13 and 14.

this way that we are able to grasp the all-inclusive nature and the full extent of our union with Christ. Our self-identity moves past what we once were into a new identity. Norman Grubb described this as "Christ in Tom's form."[28] This is simply emphasising what Paul talked about in Galatians 2:20: *"I am crucified with Christ: nevertheless I live; yet not I, but Christ liveth in me."* This is the central point to grasp! To live from this "Christ as me" reality is, in effect, to know that it is no longer I who live but *"Christ liveth in me."* Indeed, Paul expressed this thought in several ways when he said, *"Christ who is my life"*,[29] *"To me to live is Christ"*,[30] *"Much more being reconciled, we shall be saved by His life."*[31] Jesus Himself said, *"I am the way, the truth, and the life."*[32] Outside of Christ operating within we are lost as we cannot separate Christ from "His life." That is to say, "His life" is not something He gives as something separate from Himself. The only way we can have "His life" is to have Christ Himself living "His life" in us, for us, and as us by the Holy Spirit.

That makes our union with Christ the key to our life-transforming experience. Now, the Spirit of Christ, united to our spirit, energises and transforms everything. Can we identify the sugar once it's been mixed with the tea or remove the milk from the coffee or separate the sand from the cement? Of course not! All the ingredients are so joined as to become one in a brand new entity. Yet neither have ceased to be what they were. We can no longer identify which part is sugar and which part is tea or which part is milk and which is coffee or sand and cement. Each ingredient in the mixture has become one in the overall mix of the whole. We cannot tell where one ends and another begins! In the union of our spirit with Christ's Spirit we have become *"one Spirit."*[33] Identification of which part is Christ's Spirit and which part our human spirit is impossible. Why? Because there is no separation.

---

28 Quoted from Infinite Supply by Norman Grubb, chapter 3, pg. 11.
29 Colossians 3:4
30 Philippians 1:21
31 Romans 5:10
32 John 14:6
33 1 Corinthians 6:17

We and Christ are "one Spirit," and that is now our glorious, central, foundational reality. We cannot get any closer to HIM than that!

This is a paradox of course. It is difficult to grasp with our natural, logical mind as there seems to be a contradiction here. That may be one reason why Paul called it a *"mystery."* It goes against our logic to accept that two can become one and yet for there still to be a duality present, each party retaining their inherent distinctive characteristics. *"… The mystery that has been kept hidden for ages and generations, but is now disclosed to the Lord's people. To them God has chosen to make known among the Gentiles the glorious riches of this mystery, which is Christ in you, the hope of glory"* (Colossians 1:26-27 NIV).

"The hope of Glory"—What does this mean? Second Thessalonians 2:14 gives us the answer. *"It was to this end that He called you through our Gospel, so that you may obtain and share in the glory of our Lord Jesus Christ"*(AMPC). Here, we discover that we have been so joined to Christ that we share in His glory. However, what is the glory of the Lord Jesus Christ? The answer to that is clearly stated in the Lord's prayer in John 17:21-23, *"That they all may be one; as thou, Father, art in Me, and I in Thee, that they also may be one in Us … the glory which Thou gavest Me I have given them; that they may be one, even as We are one: I in them, and Thou in Me, that they may be made perfect in one."* This glory we have been given is that we share in the same glory which Jesus enjoys which, according to this verse, is to share in the union He has with the Father. Jesus, as He prays here, expresses His heartfelt desire and longing that we might become one with Him and with the Father and, as a natural consequence, with each other. Union is at the very heart of the Lord's prayer! Is there any chance that His prayer wasn't answered? I think not!

Does this relate to a corporate union? Of course, that is the larger reality. It applies to all who are born again as part of the body of Christ, but it cannot apply within a corporate understanding unless it first applies to each member individually.[34] The larger application can only be true because it firstly applies to each individual believer. Like the spokes of a wheel, each spoke joined to the center. Each new, born-again child of God is united as one to Christ. To use the same analogy Jesus used, we individually are a branch of the vine. The source of the rivers of living water is now activated and in full flow from the inside out.

So, the union we share with Christ, we share with the Father. This is how our sonship is established and the lifelong consequences of living as an orphan are replaced by the reality of being authentic sons and daughters who have their Father's DNA. We have been *"born ... of incorruptible seed."*[35] We have been restored to the conscious enjoyment of the Father's presence. What an amazing, indescribable reality!

This should not surprise us, though, as this is how Jesus defined "eternal life." We read, *"Now this is eternal life: that they may know You, the only true, supreme and sovereign God, and in the same manner know Jesus as the Christ whom You have sent"* (John 17:3 AMPC). "Eternal life" is here defined as to know experientially, in a deep and intimate way, the Father and the Son, not one or the other but both. The word "know" here in the Greek is *ginōskō*, which originally was a Jewish idiom for sexual union. Ephesians 5 then says, *"For this reason a man shall leave his father and his mother and shall be joined to his wife, and the two shall become one flesh. This mystery is very great, but I speak concerning the relation of Christ and the church"* (Ephesians 5:31-32 AMPC). Paul here is showing the interplay that exists between a husband and his wife. As a result of sexual union, they become one flesh. He then parallels this "one flesh" reality with the union that exists between Christ and the church, a Spirit-with-spirit union becoming "one spirit."

---

34 This alone is the one authentic "ecumenical movement." Not a man-made union of structure, theology, or governance, but of life, one Spirit, one organism! It includes all who are born of the Spirit and excludes everyone else.
35 1 Peter 1:23

Peter even tells us our humanity now participates in the benefits of the divine nature in a way we could never have imagined. "*Whereby are given unto us exceeding great and precious promises: that by these ye might be partakers of the divine nature ...*" (2 Peter 1:4). "Self," no longer our source but dependent on its union with Christ, becomes a "new self" and a partaker of the divine nature. To be a "partaker of the divine nature" is to be a partaker of the boundless, infinite riches that are "in Christ." We see the exact same thought expressed in this verse: "*Neither circumcision nor uncircumcision means anything; what counts is the new creation*" (Galatians 6:15 NIV). In other words, keeping law or not keeping law is no longer the relevant issue as it had been over many centuries. Union with Christ, making us a new creation, is the only thing that counts.

This is a profound "mystery" but also a wonderful and glorious reality which lifts our fallen, broken humanity out of the quagmire of our orphaned desolation. It grounds our identity firmly on the rock of true "sonship," separating us from all the brokenness, emptiness, and lack that once held us captive. We are now home; we are back in our Father's house. Indeed, living out of the reality of our union with Christ is the linchpin that activates the fullness of Christ in us, so He consistently lives His fullness through us and as us. This is rest! This is the summit of God's loving plan of redemption. It is the end of all separation! It is the grand centrepiece of the Good News, the essence of the New Covenant. Christ, in all that He is, His limitless, endless indescribable resources, now eternally united to us in all our enfeebled, weakened, and deficient "self." It will take the rest of eternity to explore even in part the implications of this wonderful reality! Indeed, it is as we become more stable in this walk that we make the startling discovery that there are no longer two wills competing for supremacy within us, there is only one will. With all our heart His will has become our will. That is the very essence of union! That's not to say we can't get pulled away and follow other superficial distractions from time to time, but at our core all we long for with every fibre of our being is HIM and to see His will being done "on earth as it is in heaven" to the fullest possible extent.

As this new reality begins to dawn on us, faith can be activated so that we increasingly start to see ourselves for what we actually are—a 'new self." A new species of "self" has been born! Our spirit, our inner "I" which uniquely defines who and what we are, is no longer what it was. It is now a compound of our spirit with Christ's Spirit united into one new entity. As a result, a brand "new self" now resides at our address! This is where our minds can start to be renewed, our foundational perspective of who we are and how we operate starts to change. We are now *"growing up into Christ who is our head"* (Eph 4:15), not theologically but functionally. We discover a new dimension from which we can live our lives so that we can start to *"reign in life through the one man Jesus Christ"* (Romans 5:17 ESV).

That is how the "new creation," "new self" operates. Life is no longer dictated by circumstance or the limits of our own ability and effort but by our union with Him, by His resources, by His purposes and His Kingdom now activated in our life. In other words, "His good, pleasing and perfect will"[36] begins to be manifest in the cut and thrust of our daily lives. Not as though we were robots but as joint participants sharing together in a common life and because of that, a common purpose. We become co-workers together with Him.[37] Christ is now our source of life and our supply in life.

Paul's astonishing statement moves from a theoretical one into practical experience: *"Therefore if any man be in Christ, he is a new creature: old things are passed away; behold, all things are become new"* (2 Corinthians 5:17). Then he lifts us into an even higher level in Romans 8:15-17. He says, *"We are the children of God: And if children, then heirs; heirs of God, and joint-heirs with Christ."* Think about that! That perfectly defines our new identity. We have become fully fledged children of God, heirs of deity, by becoming one spirit with Christ and, as a result, with the Father. What more could a loving Father do to recover His fallen, broken humanity?

---

36 Romans 8:2
37 1 Corinthians 3:9

A.W. Pink, said, *"The subject of spiritual union is the most important, the most profound, and yet the most blessed of any that is set forth in the sacred Scriptures; and yet, sad to say, there is hardly any which is now more generally neglected. The very expression, "spiritual union," is unknown in most professing Christian circles, and even where it is employed, it is given such a protracted meaning as to take in only a fragment of this precious truth."*[38]

T. Austin Sparks, that well-known evangelist and author, made this statement: *"Union with Christ is the heart or centre of all that has been revealed of God's thought concerning man and of man's relationship to God. Union with Christ is like the hub of a mighty wheel."*[39]

A.W. Tozer said this: *"The Spirit of God has impelled me to preach and write much about the believer's conscious union with Christ—a union that must be felt and experienced. I will never be through talking about the union of the soul with the Savior, the conscious union of the believer's heart with Jesus. Remember, I am not talking about a "theological union" only. I am speaking also of a conscious union, a union that is felt and experienced."*[40]

I have discovered that our union with Christ is the fountain head from which the mighty torrent of the ever-flowing river of divine life flows into our lives. God's plan to recover His fallen children is to bring us into union with Christ. Hebrews describes this truth by saying we are *"made partakers of Christ"* (Hebrews 3:14). If we can get even a glimpse of what it means to be "a partaker of Christ," it will radically change our view of ourselves and transform our lives. This cannot be surpassed! We have become a people who now operate out of a fixed union with the divine nature.

---

38 From A.W. Pink's book Spiritual Union and Communion, Baker 1971, pg 7, credited by some as being one of the most influential evangelical authors in the second half of the twentieth century.
39 From T. Austin Spark's book Union With Christ.
40 Quoted by A. W. Tozer in his sermon "United with Christ" available on *sermonindex.net* under Text Sermons.

The most profound truth is that He has drawn us in our fallen, broken humanity into HIS very "SELF"! This is our amazing, glorious reality! Now we understand, in part at least, what it means for our lives to be *"hidden in union with Christ in God"* (Colossians 3:3). We are united with divinity, the Father and the Son, through the Spirit, whilst still walking the streets of our broken cities.[41]

---

41 I have mentioned just a few names who will be recognised by many as devout and highly credible Bible teachers who put union with Christ at the very centre of their biblical theology. Sufficient I hope to show this is not a fringe doctrine or a recently concocted theology. Indeed, it can be traced back to the writings of the early church fathers, such as Irenaeus, Athanasius, and Augustine. Luther and Calvin also ardently expounded the centrality of Union with Christ. John Owen, Jonathan Edwards, and more recently Karl Barth and C S Lewis also wrote about Union with Christ as did Dietrich Bonhoeffer and more recently TF Torrance. That's not to say their understanding of it may not have differed in certain aspects.

Chapter 15

Branch Life Is Union Life

As the Holy Spirit begins to open our eyes to the fact that we are not the same person we once were, we embark on a progressive realisation that dismantles our false consciousness of separation from our divine source. Previously all of us have known "self" awareness, perhaps some have also intermittently known "Christ" awareness but operating in parallel to each other or side by side if you like. Now, the reality of our union with Christ results in a discernible, abiding sense of a dual consciousness where "self" consciousness operates out of "Christ" consciousness in a wonderful "oneness" with each other. This realisation pushes us across that final line where there is no longer any separation between "Christ" and "self." A union of identity has taken place. The gap has been closed! How much closer to Him could we get?

Every day can now be lived increasingly from this perspective. *"No longer I but Christ"* (Galatians 2:20), becomes the rock beneath our feet, the basis from which we go to work, from which we play and from which we live. Now we naturally and effortlessly grow into a sense of completeness and oneness with the inexhaustible supply which is Christ. This brings us into a place where we find ourselves operating out of adequacy and sufficiency, no longer out of lack. To use a computer analogy again, this is the manufacturer's new operating system now installed and running within.

As we bask in this truth and allow the Holy Spirit to expand this reality within our consciousness it reframes our thinking and disarms all our limitations and demolishes every barrier. This truth changes everything about ourselves. It not only alters our identity of who and what we are internally but it also alters our view of our external life. Living from this posture is rest and peace since we partake in all of the benefits of His divine nature now living our life. We are now co-joined to divinity.

In my experience, this truth of our union with Christ has become the corner stone for everything. It is the door through which the mighty transforming presence of an omnipotent God is released within us by His Spirit. It is the one all encompassing answer to everything!

Of course, the early stages of our walk are characterised by the analogy Paul used of "earthen vessels" or containers. The container analogy is emphasising that we are containers that contain the fulness of divinity. We are not on our own. Heaven has come down to us. As wonderful as this is, it is also as much as we can grasp in a functional way prior to the realisation of union. It is only as we come into the enjoyment of our union with Christ that we then move into the experience of the second analogy Jesus talked about—of branches joined to the vine.

This analogy in John 15, that we are branches united to the vine, reflects who we are in union with Christ. It loses none of the emphasis we learned as containers but it goes on to emphasise that our source for all we could possibly need, for all we will ever become, and for all we do is not in ourselves but in the Vine. The Passion Translation puts this very well: *"So you must remain in life-union with me, for I remain in life-union with you. For as a branch severed from the vine will not bear fruit, so your life will be fruitless unless you live your life intimately joined to mine. I am the sprouting vine and you're my branches. As you live in union with me as your source, fruitfulness will stream from within you—but when you live separated from me you are powerless. ... When your lives bear abundant fruit, you demonstrate that you are my mature disciples who glorify my Father!"* (John 15:4-8 TPT).

This "branch life" analogy expresses "union life" in all its fullness. There is no gap between the branch and the vine. They are one! This is the "new creation life" in a nutshell. Rest and refreshment, effortless fruitfulness, and our Father being glorified in our lives are all by-products of one thing and one thing only: *"abiding in the vine."* Such a simple thing to do but what an amazing outcome. Fruit grows as a by-product of us stepping out of "self" and all its best endeavours into the enjoyment of our union with Christ as our total supply for every aspect of our lives.

So what does it mean to "abide in the vine" and how do we do that? There are several facets to what it means practically speaking. The central lesson of this analogy is that the branch and the vine are one. The branch does not act independently from the vine, nor can it sustain or support itself. That means that the essence of "abiding" is found in resting in the vine, or *"entering God's rest"* and *"ceasing from its own works"* (Hebrews 4:10). We simply allow ourselves to be upheld and sustained by the vine and continue to "abide" in that posture. We remain dependent on His indwelling presence. "Self" is no longer in control and has no independent role to play. Like Paul, we have discovered what it means to *"put no confidence in the flesh"* (Philippians 3:3). This inevitably tips us over into the only other option open to us: utter dependence on Christ Himself within. This means that *"abiding in the vine"* can only happen when we come to the end of dependence on our own resources and effort. Paul, describing how he lived this life, said he lived it *"by faith in [by adherence to and reliance on and complete trust in] the Son of God, Who loved me and gave Himself up for me"* (Galatians 2:20 AMPC). We can see, therefore, that faith, that is, reliance and dependence on Christ in us, to live His life through us, is the main characteristic of "abiding."

This is the necessary step-change because a branch has no life of its own and it cannot survive on its own. Jesus said, *"Without me ye can do nothing."* [42] Nothing! Nothing can never become something no matter

---

42 John 15:5

how hard we try! This is the end of "self's" contribution. In a natural vine the sap continually and effortlessly flows into the branches so long as they remain connected to the vine. A branch does not work to extract the sap, it is provided freely by the vine through the union the branch has to the vine. The vine is the source of sustenance and life and the means by which the branch is nourished and sustained causing it to produce good fruit. It is no different for us. Jesus ties our usefulness and fruitfulness directly to this single requirement of "abiding in the vine." Indeed, the promise is of "much fruit."

Therefore, to *"abide in the vine"* is to live in union with *"Christ who is our life"* (Colossians 3:4). We learn that "abiding" is resting on the continual flow of an inner life not our own. The resurrection power of the resurrected Christ spontaneously and continually springs up and overflows from within so long as we "abide." This was what Jesus promised us in John 7:38, *"He that believeth on Me,* (a continual act) *as the Scripture hath said, out of his belly shall flow rivers of living water."* Notice that there is only one activity required for this river to flow, if it can be called an activity. We just need to depend and "believe" on Him. We can therefore dispense with all the "Christian" formulae, procedures, and protocols that we have been told are necessary for us to prime the pump so that we can squeeze the sap out of the vine by our own efforts. The fullness of the divine sap flows freely from within as we daily depend on Him. Romans 1:17 puts it like this: *"The just shall live by faith."* This is the "new self" in action!

His resources now become our resources. In other words, the divine sap flows and produces "much fruit." Our internal reality is, *"No longer I who live but Christ ... "* (Galatians 2:20). Inwardly we know we have become partakers of the divine nature (2 Peter 1:4). Indeed, our identity is one where we now see ourselves as *"partakers of Christ"* Himself (Hebrews 3:14 AMPC). So we now gladly rest in the operation of the *"law of the Spirit of life"* (Romans 8:2) which is operating within.

Our "Self"identity can then progressively move from what, for some, could be described as a "Christian-forgiven self." For others it may even be a "Christ-in-me-self," but now we move to the summit of a settled experience of a "Christ-as-me-self."[43] This becomes the basic, fixed, unchanging reality through which we interpret our internal and external experience of everyday life. That, I believe, is the first aspect of how we "abide in the vine."

The second but equally vital facet of "abiding" flows from the first. It is a simple, ongoing "acknowledgement" of the first. This is where we "abide" in what already is. It's not so much an activity as it is living out of the recognition of who we have become. We "abide" by recognising that we are branches united to the vine, that the branch is upheld by the vine and has its source in the vine. It is simply to acknowledge that this "Christ as me" reality is who I am and this fact will never change. Our inner reality is that we are now one with Christ, and we recognise that fact in the daily cut and thrust of life.

Paul said it this way, *"As ye have therefore received Christ Jesus the Lord, so walk ye in him"* (Colossians 2:6) or as Romans 13:14 says *"Put ye on the Lord Jesus Christ."* That means we see ourselves for who and what we now are, recognising that Christ Himself is our life, our source, and our supply for everything we will ever need. We "walk in Him," united to Him and dependent on Him and on His activity in us and through us. The branch does not act independently from the trunk.

This is not a passive posture however, it is a posture that continually acknowledges His Presence, His priority and Lordship. Every pull of temptation to act independently either in good deeds or evil deeds is purposely brought back into submission to Him. It is a ongoing posture of acknowledging our lives have been turned over to the operation and

---

43 Although altered by me, this form of expression was coined by Norman Grubb. He had a unique ability to bring together concepts around identity and function in a simple and straight forward manner. We find many examples of this in his book "No Independent Self". (Zerubabel Press)

Lordship of the Holy Spirit. Our wellbeing is completely tied to the trunk! This is "abiding"!

In my experience this ongoing acknowledgement of who we have become seems to be the point where the enemy attacks us the most. We are often tempted to move back into that autonomous "old self" resourced, "separated" mindset again. This usually happens because our "inner knowing," that inner witness of our union with Christ, has been compromised in some way. The world, satan, and our own un-renewed mindset can temporarily cause us to forget our true identity in union with Christ. When we do that, "Self" regains control, which in turn gets us back in that "performance" or "striving" mindset again. That is because now we see ourselves operating out of "separation" and "lack". We have lost that inner witness that we are "complete in Him." Our eyes are back on "self" and on all our "issues" rather than our new identity in Christ.

That sense of "separation" is a lie of the enemy which can get us into all sorts of bother because now the starting point of our interaction and walk with the Lord negates our true position of being in a vital union connection with Christ. We then go round and round in circles looking for more because now we are operating out of lack. What has happened is that we have allowed ourselves to be talked out of our new identity in Christ, out of our enjoyment of union with the fullness of the living Christ within us, living as us in all the "exceeding riches" of who He is in Himself, our total all-inclusive resource from which we live.

In effect we are back in "Self." In our hearts we have become disconnected from the vine and the branch starts to wither. Now all we can contribute to this walk, any ability or effort we employ, can only ever originate from "Self." We have no strength or resource within ourselves that does not originate in "Self" and so to continue down this road is no more than religion, a fake substitute for the operation of the authentic life of Christ within. I cannot overstate how subtle this is and yet how detrimental an influence it exerts on our walk.

There is a maturing aspect to what I'm saying. John describes the three stages of growth in the Christian life as "little children," then "young men," and then "fathers." Paul told the Corinthians it was time that they were able to eat solid food but they were only able to drink milk. The reality is we have to learn in our experience the difference between the two options open to us. We start to experience what it is to live from our "new self" identity and how it differs from living from our "old self" identity. That is, we start to recognise inwardly when we are walking in the "Spirit" and when we are walking in "Self" or "Flesh." "Self" is insidious and will always seek to regain control, especially religious "self." Nevertheless, over time the hedges on both sides of this road become clear and inwardly more defined.

Hudson Taylor founded the China Inland Mission in 1865. He was a spiritual giant mightily used by God in China. In a letter to his sister back in England he penned these words.[44] *"The Spirit of God revealed to me the truth of our oneness with Jesus as I had never known it before. ... As I thought of the Vine and the branches, what light the blessed Spirit poured direct into my soul! How great seemed my mistake in wishing to get the sap, the fullness out of Him! I saw not only that Jesus will never leave me, but that I am a member of His body, of His flesh and of His bones. ... It is a wonderful thing to be really one with a risen and exalted Saviour, to be a member of Christ! Think what it involves. Can Christ be rich and I poor? Can your right hand be rich and your left poor? Or your head be well fed while your body starves? The sweetest part... is the rest which full identification with Christ brings. I am no longer anxious about anything, as I realise this; for He, I know, is able to carry out His will, and His will is mine. It makes no matter where He places me, or how. No fear that His resources will prove unequal to any emergency! And His resources are mine,*

---

44 Readily available on internet. Also available on Scribd.com/document117541864/Letter-to-sister-The-Exchanged-Life-Hudson-Taylor

for He is mine, and is with me and dwells in me. And since Christ has thus dwelt in my heart by faith, how happy I have been! ... I am no better than before. In a sense, I do not wish to be, nor am I striving to be. But I am dead and buried with Christ, ay, and risen too! And now Christ lives in me, and 'the life that I now live in the flesh, I live by faith of the Son of God, who loved me and gave Himself for me." We can detect here how real his union with Christ was to him as it oozes out in every syllable, word and sentence!

To summarise then, to *"abide in the vine"* is to *"walk in the Spirit"* and the doorway into "walking in the Spirit" is only opened when "self" comes to the end of itself and ceases to be the source from which we operate. This means it doesn't primarily operate at the level of our intellect where He commands and we do our level best to obey. Nor is it where we are constrained to precariously walk a tightrope called "His will," and we try to obey out of duty or some sense of loyalty or even enlightened self-interest. That would be a symptom that we are still operating out of separation and "self" management.[45] Indeed, "abiding" in the reality that His life has become our life is the key to everything! Christ HIMself—not theology, not Bible knowledge, not meetings but the indwelling Christ—has become our life. The rivers of peace and joy then overflow and unrestrained pleasure and delight well up unchecked from within. The indescribable joy of "Christ as me"[46] banishes all fear, dread, and lack.

We now live from the inside out with increasing confidence, fully expressing what is in our hearts. We discover the wonderful freedom that comes from having gotten ourselves out of our own hands. This is the outworking of the liberating life-altering truth, that *"If the Son therefore shall make you free, ye shall be free indeed"* (John 8:36).

---

45 There is a world of difference between a "self-management" which expresses an autonomous "self," acting on its own from a self-resourced, self-reliant perspective and the necessary "self-management" which is a response to our dependence on the Holy Spirit's activity within us.

46 This term was coined by Norman Grubb, sometimes personalised as "Christ as me." Used in several of his books such as No Independent Self, Zerubbel Press, pg. 13 and 14.

So we see that the Father's total provision for His children is Christ in them, living as them. It is nothing less than the fullness of Christ Himself united to our spirit within by the Holy Spirit. He is the ultimate, all-conquering King and, in His loving outpouring of Himself into our feeble empty vessels, He undertakes to do all and provide for all. Abiding in the reality of our union with Christ is the means by which we escape all the debilitating, energy-sapping, frustration of life being lived by reliance on "Self." It flings wide the floodgates, ushering us into the sunlit uplands of the divine ecosystem of the Kingdom of God. Here, we enjoy His limitless resources and discover an overflow of adequacy and sufficiency flowing in our lives. We find satisfaction in the reality of our new identity in union with Christ. Peace and rest now reigns within.

Chapter 16

"Abiding" Is Living "Through Him"

We have talked about union with Christ and what it means to "abide" in Him so that His Presence becomes our daily constant. We now see ourselves as branches of the divine vine and, going forward, our life and spiritual growth is defined by our "abiding" in that reality. Jesus said, *"For without me ye can do nothing. If a man abide not in me, he is cast forth as a branch, and is withered"* (John 15:5-6). From that we learn that remaining in union with the Vine is our key to life as God intended us to live it. So what does life look like from an "abiding" perspective?

We have a wonderful example of someone who lived His life out of "union" with His Father. Jesus did not hide the source from which He Himself operated and which equipped Him so thoroughly and so completely. He lifted the veil on His inner adequacy and union with the Father when He said, *"I and my Father are one"* (John 10:30). Then again: *"He that hath seen me hath seen the Father; and how sayest thou then, Shew us the Father? ... The words that I speak unto you I speak not of myself: but the Father that dwelleth in me, He doeth the works"* (John 14:7-11). Here, Jesus is confirming not just His union with the Father but also that the source of His words and actions were not in Himself but in the Father. Jesus was not the source of the miracles; ultimately it was the Father who was doing the works through the Son.

Indeed, Jesus said He could do nothing out of "Self" even though He was the Son of God. John 5:19 says, *"Most solemnly I say to you, the Son can do nothing of Himself, unless it is something He sees the Father doing."* Then later in the same chapter, *"I can do nothing on my own initiative or authority"* (John 5:30 AMPC). This is our pattern for how life is to be lived in union with Christ. To the natural mind, this is hard to comprehend as many of us are so utterly immersed in "self" generated, "self" reliant activity that we cannot easily understand how it could be otherwise.

We see this was how Paul functioned as we read in Galatians, *"Nevertheless I live; yet not I, but Christ liveth in me"* (Galatians 2:20). Also *"but I laboured more abundantly than they all: yet not I, but the grace of God which was with me"* (1 Corinthians 15:10). These verses make it clear that Paul was not independently trying to work "for God." For him it was not a career choice nor was he simply fulfilling what was on his schedule or calendar. Rather, as he put it, *"For this I labor, striving with all the superhuman energy which He so mightily enkindles and works within me"* (Colossians 1:28-29 AMPC). We see, in effect, that His humanity had become a channel through which the indwelling Christ now expressed Himself.

John then applies this same pattern to us in 1 John 4:9: *"In this the love of God was made manifest [displayed] where we are concerned: in that God sent His Son, the only begotten or unique [Son], into the world so that we might live through Him"* (AMPC). Our Father's total provision for us is His Son as we learn what it means functionally to *"live through Him."*

Jesus then explicitly reinforces this same principle in John 6:57: *"Just as the living Father sent Me and I live by [through] the Father, even so whoever continues to feed on Me [whoever takes Me for his food and is nourished by Me] shall [in his turn] live through and because of Me"* (AMPC). Firstly, He reveals to us His own "modus operandi" by saying He lived "through" the Father but then applies that same principle to us, stating that we are to live our life "through" Him. That is, simply living in dependence on His dynamic operation and presence within.

Living our lives "through Him" lifts us up to live on a higher plain. We now operate out of rest, always recognising our total dependence on the indwelling Christ for every area of our lives. As we *"grow up into him in all things, which is the head, even Christ"* (Ephesians 4:15), we become a channel though which the divine life is expressed.

Paul then defined the limitless possibilities for those who live this life in Philippians 4:13: *"I have strength for all things in Christ Who empowers me [I am ready for anything and equal to anything through Him Who infuses inner strength into me; I am self-sufficient in Christ's sufficiency]"* (AMPC).

That effectively means that our limitations are superseded by a higher dynamic at work in us. To live life "through Him" from this "new self," "new identity" posture is to "walk in the Spirit." In effect, this is like learning to walk on water. We can never do that, at least not out of our own resources, yet we see Peter did exactly that for a brief time. The Lord encouraged Him to get out of the boat, to get out of that man-made craft that was the product of human ingenuity and self-effort, and to walk in a way that was far beyond his own natural ability. Yes, it was Peter who climbed out of the boat, it was Peter who expended the energy of putting one leg in front of the other as he walked on the water, but it was not Peter who kept himself afloat on the surface of the water. For a short time, he stepped into a different realm of operation where he would be sustained and upheld by resources that were not his own. Likewise, it is we who go into the office, drive the tractor, or do whatever we do in our everyday lives but it is not our resources or our ability or our effort that sustains us any longer. We are in a new realm now! It is the mighty, omnipotent Spirit ever flowing from within who keeps us and holds us and sustains us. We settle down into a deep, implicit dependence on the living, dynamic presence of Christ within.

That is how we escape the natural life, the "self" or "flesh" life, the life where we are sustained by our own efforts and natural resources.

From the outside it may appear to others as though nothing has changed but inside we know differently. Andrew Murray put it like this: *"Our life is to be a life of perfect union with Jesus. Many people look upon Christ as a separate, outward Savior. ... He is here in me, His branch. He comes into my inmost life, He occupies that life, He lives there, and by living there He enables me to live as a child of God. Christ comes into me and becomes my very life. He comes into the very root of my heart and being. He comes into my willing and thinking and feeling and living, and lives in me in the power which the Omnipresent God alone can exercise."*[47]

Major Ian Thomas described this walk by saying, *"If you are to know the fullness of the life of Christ, you are to appropriate the efficacy of what He is in the same way as you have already appropriated the efficacy of what He has done."* He then goes on, *"Relate everything, moment by moment, as it arises to the adequacy of what He is in you, and assume that His adequacy will be operative. What satisfies Him is to see me, in every situation, bowing myself out and bowing Him in, saying, 'Without you I am nothing and can do nothing, I now rest in you to do it.'"*[48] Although this seems to be expressed here as a formula, it is simply living from the acknowledgement of our new internal reality. Paul expressed the same thought in Ephesians 6:10: *"In conclusion, be strong in the Lord, be empowered through your union with Him; draw your strength from Him, that strength which His boundless might provide"* (AMPC). To *"draw our strength from Him"* is simply to lean into His life and depend on His operation within, knowing that "His adequacy" is active and flowing in us and through us. Proverbs even rounds this out for us. *"Roll your works upon the Lord [commit and trust them wholly to Him; He will cause your thoughts to become agreeable to His will, and] so shall your plans be*

47 Andrew Murray, missionary in South Africa and prolific author during the mid to late 19th century. This quote is from his book The Spiritual Life.
48 Major Ian Thomas, evangelist, author and founder of *Capernwray Missionary Fellowship of Torchbearers*, describes how we operate from this new reality in his book The Indwelling Life of Christ, pg 137.

established and succeed" (Proverbs 16:3 AMPC). Proverbs 3 reinforces the same point: *"Trust in the LORD with all thine heart; And lean not unto thine own understanding. In all thy ways acknowledge Him, And He shall direct thy paths"* (Proverbs 3:5-6).

On the surface we continue to function in all the areas of our lives very much as we did before. We take all our responsibilities and relationships seriously and are thoroughly professional in our approach to our work. We employ all our knowledge, training, and talent and may work just as hard as we ever did. The difference is that now our confidence is no longer based on what WE can do but in Him. We discover in a functional way that He's got us, and He is our source for everything. Paul told us the source of his strength when he said, *"Not that we are fit [qualified and sufficient in ability] of ourselves to form personal judgments or to claim or count anything as coming from us, but our power and ability and sufficiency are from God"* (2 Corinthians 3:5 AMPC). This applies both to what is going on inside us as much as in the outer circumstances of our lives.

This radically contrasts with a "self-managed" Christianity operating out of a "separated" mindset. That is as far removed as we can be from a Spirit-managed, Spirit-empowered, Spirit-led Spirit-union where the power of His resurrection has been released within us and Christ is now our life. The delusion of "self"-improvement is a relic of our old life. Indeed, the very definition of legalism is depending on anything we do as a work in order to make progress in our Christian walk or to gain ground spiritually. This "effort-based" "works" thinking betrays the fact that we, or should I say, the "old self" is still in control and still labouring under the illusion that it can make progress by managing our spirituality using spiritual tools and implementing learnt spiritual disciplines. Now, it is no longer we who hold onto Christ by the quality of our commitment and diligent effort. Why? Because dependency is the only thing we have left once we have been awakened to the futility of our own resources and come to the end of ourselves. Christ alone is now everything to us! We have entered God's rest and rely on Christ's indwelling presence to do what we could never do.

The liberating truth is that we belong to Christ and *"He who has begun a good work in you will [continue to] perfect and complete it until the day of Christ Jesus [the time of His return]"* (Philippians 1:6 AMPC). He will see to it that we do *"the works that He has predestined in advance that we should walk in."* Our posture is firmly settled now. *"Looking away [from all that will distract] to Jesus, Who is the Leader and the Source of our faith [giving the first incentive for our belief] and is also its Finisher [bringing it to maturity and perfection]* (Hebrews 12:2 AMPC), Philippians 2:13 spells the same truth out for us in clear, uncompromising terms: *"Not in your own strength for it is God Who is all the while effectually at work in you, energising and creating in you the power and desire, both to will and to work for His good pleasure and satisfaction and delight"* (AMPC). Notice the little phrase *"all the while"* in this verse. This is a continual, transforming flow! The entire premise of the New Covenant and where it differs from the Old Covenant is the same promise of effortless transformation. The promise of the coming New Covenant in Ezekiel 36:26-27 says, *"A new heart will I give you and a new spirit will I put within you, and I will take away the stony heart out of your flesh and give you a heart of flesh. And I will put My Spirit within you and cause you to walk in My statutes, and you shall heed My ordinances and do them"* (AMPC). Notice the phrase, *"I will cause you to walk in My statutes."* This totally removes the pressure to perform and improve ourselves even if we could.

The burden now rolls off our shoulders of continually trying to live the Christian life. It is from our experience of abiding in union with the risen Christ that we discover that unforced change begins to happen from within, altering our desires and conduct. We find an inner adequacy, a resource we didn't know before, equipping us and fitting us to live life on a different plane. He enables us to live spontaneously and authentically in the experience of all that He is in us. His life, not "self" is now our source. *"I live; yet not I, but Christ lives in me!* (Galatians 2:20). He now expresses HIMself as a natural outflow of who we now are: a "new self" in union with Christ. This is described in Jude: *"To him who is able to keep you from stumbling and to present you before His glorious presence without fault and with great joy ..."* (Jude 1:24 NIV). Notice, if we have abandoned ourselves into His keeping it is He who is keeping us, not we ourselves. It is He who will present us *"without fault"* to the Father.

That being the case, we must ask ourselves, how then should we understand "law" and "rule keeping" and do these still play a role in the life of a New Covenant believer? Having received forgiveness as a free gift, many still approach the New Testament with a similar mindset to Old Covenant believers. They relate to a separated "Christ" and see all the numerous instructions and precepts outlined in the New Testament as rules they need to keep out of their own independent "self's" ability and efforts. Compliance with these rules then become the measuring stick by which they judge spiritual progress.

However, to attempt to keep any precept or directive out of "Self" effort is no different to operating under the Old Covenant "law" keeping principle. The New Covenant is very different. It does not make demands from the outside. It speaks to the "new self" alone, this "new creation" identity, which as we have seen, functions and walks out of dependence on its union with Christ with a "through Him" dynamic.

How could it be otherwise since we have already seen that, from God's perspective, "Self" has been crucified with Christ and has died as an independent source from which we live? How then could God place any demand on it? "Self" has been utterly rejected as a resource for pleasing God. That applies whether we are saved or not. That way is diametrically opposed to the operation of the New Covenant. Paul shares with us what he discovered when he was trying to do the right thing out of "Self." In Romans 7:21 he tells us that it was when he *"would do good"* that he found only *"evil was present"* in himself.

This tips us over into an obedience that springs from faith, not works or self-effort. Paul said, *"... but has now been disclosed and through the prophetic writings has been made known to all nations, according to the command of the eternal God, to bring about the obedience of faith"* (Romans 16:26 ESV). Jesus, in Book of Acts put it like this: *"... so that they may receive forgiveness of sins and a place among those who are sanctified by faith in me"* (Acts 26:18 NIV). Note, we *"are sanctified by faith in Him,"* not by self-resourced rule-keeping and works. To be sanctified is to be made inwardly holy, that is, for our desires to be brought into alignment with God's desires. We move from external rules and Law-keeping to operating out of desire and delight in doing what pleases HIM. This is pure freedom, not duty! Christ now within, in all His beautiful personhood, has won our hearts. His influences and operation alters us at the very basic level of our being.

Galatians puts it this way: *"So then, those who are of faith are blessed along with Abraham, the man of faith. For all who rely on works of the Law are under a curse"* (Galatians 3:7, 9-10 ESV). Isn't that a fearfully chilling statement? So, to rely *"on works of the Law,"* which is self-resourced self-effort, either as a means for starting the Christian life or for living it, is to come under a curse. Furthermore, to find ourselves back under Law, according to Galatians 5:4, is to discover that we are effectively *"alienated," "separated,"* or *"severed from Christ,"* depending on which Bible translation you use.

Scripture makes it clear that for those who are born of the Spirit there is no law for us to keep. Paul said, *"For I through the law am dead to the law, that I might live unto God"* (Galatians 2:19). This is saying that the sentence for us having broken the Law has been carried out and the "old self" has died as a result. So, the new birth as well as our new life is lived from the other side of the Law beyond its jurisdiction. Galatians states this explicitly: *"If you are guided (led) by the [Holy] Spirit, you are not subject to the Law"* (Galatians 5:18 AMPC). What I'm saying is, *"We have been released from Law ... so that we serve God in the newness of the Spirit and not in the oldness of the letter of the Law"* (Romans 7:6 AMPC).

What a wonderful release this is for many of us who have been brought up with such a legalistic, meritorious, and self-reliant, rule-keeping perspective of Christianity. What a freedom we come into when we realise our acceptability and continued right standing before God, as well as our ongoing daily conduct, are all the by-product of our dependence on Christ Himself within and not on "self" working and striving to keep some external code of conduct. The only precondition to this is that we continue to "abide." Our hearts are then altered by the reality of God's love for us and by our intimacy with His wonderful presence. We find ourselves wholeheartedly doing what pleases Him. We operate out of freedom and desire, not duty or Law. Indeed, now to do what pleases Him pleases us!

This is how that rule-keeping yardstick which was the source of so much condemnation and failure is completely removed. We have stepped out of "self" and abandoned ourselves to the Holy Spirit so we now rest in a moment-by-moment enabling on Him without those impossible rules and demands which previously exposed and reinforced our weakness and brokenness. Love accomplishes what LAW never could. For those who are walking in this "Christ as me"[49] reality there is no Law for us to keep.

So, we need to be on our guard and maintain our freedom for although the Law is still in operation today[50] it has no jurisdiction over those who have died to it and been resurrected with Christ by His Spirit. To live from our "new self" is to live beyond the jurisdiction of all Law, from whatever source and all forms of externally prescribed behaviour. All the impossible demands, precepts, and principles Christendom

49 This term was coined by Norman Grubb, sometimes personalised as "Christ as me." Used in several of his books such as No Independent Self, Zerubabel Press, pg. 13 and 14.
50 Matthew 5:17-18

has laboured to enforce are now removed and replaced by a person dwelling within. This person is Christ Himself, our own personified *"Law-keeper."[51]* He has taken up residence within us, and it is He who naturally and instinctively keeps "Law" in us and for us. Here, the *"Law of the Spirit of life in Christ Jesus"* does what "self" could never do. It lifts us into a realm where the *"Law of sin and death"* loosens its grip and hold over us.

Could this be the answer, in part at least, to much of the mediocrity and weakness within the Body of Christ today? It is not, as is generally thought, that our weakness stems from needing more of the Holy Spirit. Rather it is the direct consequence of our dependence on "Self" striving to live the Christian life by seeking to implement biblical principles and precepts out of our own meagre resources. The Holy Spirit didn't come to "help" us to be better or nicer people and more "Christian". He came to open our eyes to our utter weakness and brokenness so we would cast ourselves entirely on Christ to do for us what we could never do. Only those who have come to the end of "Self" and know its brokenness are able to wholeheartedly abide, on a consistent basis, in the full flow of *"the law of the Spirit of life in Christ Jesus"* (Romans 8:2). It is then that we discover the artesian well Jesus talked about which *"springs up into everlasting life"* (John 4:14).

This is our key to rest. This our route to freedom from all condemnation and guilt because how can we break a Law that no longer has jurisdiction over us? It's impossible because, for us, there is no Law to break! Indeed, the "All in All" has united Himself to us and become our own "All in All."[52] Now, there is no longer any separation from Him. There is no more need for more. There is no more striving and no more searching! That's not to say we have arrived but we have found "the pearl of great price" and it will take the rest of eternity to unravel the riches of Him

---

51 This expression of Christ as our indwelling "Law keeper" was coined by Norman Grubb. See The Intercessor, Vol 29 Number 4, article entitled "Total Salvation."
52 Colossians 3:11

who has settled us and brought such contentment into our lives. Now we abide in Him and rest on Him in all His completeness and in all He is in us, living as us. He has become our all-encompassing answer to everything!

Chapter 17

The Road to Intimacy

Intimacy is the culmination of God's love for us and His intention toward us. Therefore, in our understanding of what it means to "abide in the vine," we should also include this third facet of how we spend time in His Presence fellowshipping on purpose, enjoying the rest, refreshment, and renewal that comes from our growing intimacy with Him.

Intimacy cannot be arrived at by coercion or Law and rule-keeping! There can be no element that we "should" come or "ought" to come to Him. Now our interaction with Him is not a duty or a work we need to discharge! As husbands, how much duty is involved in loving our wives? If we are responding to the Lord out of duty or as a work, I suspect we may still be operating as I did out of a "separated," self-management mindset, still "trying" to do what we think is expected of us. Now we no longer "seek Him" as a means to an end in order to become more spiritual, more holy, or more acceptable. Christ is now all that to us. Those "self-improvement" motives belong to a previous life! Now, we just want to spend time with Him for His own sake.

The incredible reality is that once He has come to us, and we know Him as a vital, indwelling reality, His presence draws us like a magnet. We can't stay away! Psalms 84:1-2, 10 says: *"How lovely is your dwelling place, O Lord of hosts! My soul longs, yes, faints for the courts of the Lord.*

... For a day in your courts is better than a thousand elsewhere. I would rather be a doorkeeper in the house of my God than dwell in the tents of wickedness" (AMPC).

Those endless, weary days when guilt and condemnation hung over us like a suffocating, impenetrable, dark blanket are in the past. Now we know with every fibre of our being that we are loved, fully and completely accepted, perfectly qualified to come close. Why? Because He is the one who has qualified us, and He is the one who has come so very near to us. His perfect love has indeed banished all our fear. We have a witness on the inside of us which confirms that we are no longer orphans but authentic sons of our Father! *"For the Spirit which you have now received is not a spirit of slavery to put you once more in bondage to fear, but you have received the Spirit of adoption, the Spirit-producing sonship in the **bliss** of which we cry, Abba Father! Father! The Spirit Himself thus testifies together with our own spirit, assuring us that we are children of God"* (Romans 8:15-16 AMPC—bold mine).

This experience settles and completes us like nothing else can! He is now our default posture, like a well-used armchair that we fall into at the end of a busy day. We put on our slippers and relax with Him and *"sup"* with Him.[53]

We find in various books of the Old Testament the expression "waiting on God." This, to my mind is the Old Covenant expression which closely parallels this New Testament term we have been considering: *"abiding in the vine."* Many Old Testament writers describe the intimacy and joy they experienced simply resting in His presence. I stumbled on this largely forgotten secret after reading a little book by Andrew Murray entitled *Waiting on God*.[54] After that conference in Northampton I felt the Lord was drawing me into a season of "waiting on Him" and, as I did so, I began to be drawn into something I hadn't realised was even possible.

---

53 Revelation 3:20
54 Waiting on God by Andrew Murray, published by Lakeland, Marshal Morgan & Scott

I read in Psalm 46:10, *"Be still, and know that I am God."* This introduced me to the vital correlation that exists between us *"being still"* in His presence and us *"knowing."* This came across to me as a vital key. It struck me that this was referring to a "knowing" that was not the result of our intellectual application or mental activity. Yet, it carried the promise of us "knowing" or "perceiving" at a different level, which I realised was talking about our spirit level. This opens us up to an entirely new dimension of "knowing."

Then Psalm 62 reinforced this correlation with silence, *"For God alone my soul waits in silence; From Him comes my salvation"* (Psalm 62:1 AMPC). Verse 5 says, *"For God alone my soul waits in silence and quietly submits to Him, For my hope is from Him."* This, to me, went beyond just waiting on God but highlights the aspect of waiting in silence and learning to be still before the Lord. I discovered that "waiting on God" in silence is counter-intuitive, yet wonderfully rewarding. This is speaking of yielding ourselves to the Lord's very presence in a posture of inner stillness and silent abandon.

Psalm 23:2 says, *"He leads me beside still and quiet waters, he refreshes and restores my soul."* This indeed is the place of restoration and refreshment! Quiet stillness is an inner calm where we have become as still as glass, like a lake on a warm summer's day without any ripples. Psalm 94 in the Passion translation expresses this thought beautifully: *"Whenever my busy thoughts were out of control, the soothing comfort of your presence calmed me down and overwhelmed me with delight"* (Psalm 94:19 TPT).

Søren Kierkegaard, the Danish theologian,[55] speaking within the context of "seeking first the Kingdom" said, *"Man differs from the beasts in that he can speak, but in relation to God it may easily be his ruin that he is too willing to speak. In proportion as a man becomes more earnest in prayer, he has less and less to say, and in the end he is quite silent. He became*

---

55 Søren Kierkegaard was a 19th-century Danish philosopher and religious author who has been labeled by many as the "Father of Existentialism." He wrote his "Christian Discourses" in 1848. This is an extract from that work.

silent. Indeed he became, if such a thing be possible, something still more opposed to speaking than silence is. He became a hearer. He thought that to pray was to speak. He learned that prayer is not only to keep silence but to listen. And so it is. Prayer is not to hear one's self speak, but to arrive at silence, and continue being silent; to wait till one hears God speak." He then goes on, *"Not as though prayer always begins in silence, but because when prayer really has become prayer, then it has become silence—and that is what it means to seek first God's Kingdom."*

I found that insight very helpful as I had discovered there are only so many times we can ask for a thing before it becomes meaningless repetition. I found out that, as this indicates, prayer is not primarily about what comes out of our mouths, it is about what is going on in our hearts. Praying from our hearts is very different. Cerebral, intellectual prayers have their place, but it is with the heart that we encounter Him. In silence we learn to open up our inner world to Him without words. We make ourselves transparent to Him, knowing that it is the yearning of our hearts that He sees.

In practical terms then, what does it mean to "wait on God" and how can we do it within the context we are discussing? Firstly, we come just as we are, whatever our failure, no matter how distant we may feel from Him. We come because He is infinite LOVE. Just as when we sit under the warm summer sun and feel its warmth, so by waiting in His presence we encounter His unconditional love. Andrew Murray said, *"God's love is just His delight to impart Himself and His blessedness to His children."*[56]

So to "wait on God" is to find a quiet place where we can take time out to simply fix our inner gaze and attention on Christ. The key posture is one of utter dependence, handing the entirety of ourselves into His loving hands. As we "wait on God," our waiting becomes

56 From Day Eight, Waiting on God by Andrew Murray published by Lakeland, Marshal Morgan & Scott.

the highest expression of our entire dependence on Him. Andrew Murray stated in that little book that *"waiting on God is the highest possible expression of faith."*

This clearly is going to be different for everyone but go with whatever that means to you. In whatever way you "know Him" and recognise that "inner witness" within, simply be still and let your gaze rest on Him! That is all! You don't need to say anything or try to do any of the religious stuff usually associated with prayer. In my experience, the less said the better because this is not primarily about expressing our rational thoughts, this is at a heart level. It is spirit engaging with Spirit.

Simply come to Him believing that God Himself, in His infinite love for you, will reward you. *"Anyone who comes to Him must believe that He exists and that He rewards those who earnestly seek Him"* (Hebrews 11:6 NIV). Yield yourself to Him then, trusting He will draw your gaze to Himself. His inexpressively, beautiful, wonderful Presence will rise up from within. Your ability to keep your gaze fixed on Him will develop and grow as you engage with Him on an ongoing and regular basis.

When I was first drawn to this initially, it felt frustrating and unrewarding. I found it hard as my thoughts wandered so much and, sometimes, I would even fall asleep. At times my mind would inevitably get taken up with everything that was going on in my life. I found it difficult to move beyond my mental and rational activity and I felt trapped in my own thinking. Ironically, if I managed to disengage from all that was going on in my life, I found my mind would go into overdrive, taken up with biblical concepts, principles and verses of Scripture. These all combined to keep my focus away from that all important face-to-face, intimate communion with the vital presence of Christ Himself. However, the Lord had impressed on me to do this, so as I pressed in, over time, I found my ability to step beyond my own thoughts and have my mind *"stayed on Him"*[57] developed. What I discovered is that to be *"still and know"* is a learnt process!

---

57 Isaiah 26:3

As beneficiaries of the New Covenant, the doorway into the Holy of Holies has been opened up to us from within. The wonderful truth is that we have become a temple within which He already resides. We don't need to go to a meeting or any designated location to enter this hallowed place as those under the Old Covenant had to do. Neither do we need black-out blinds, dimmed lights, and soft music to lead us there. This simple but profound truth is of critical importance: To encounter Him, all we need is to retreat into our own inner chamber where His presence continually dwells!

Something else quite amazing began to happen. I discovered this was the place where we receive revelation and divine instruction. Jesus said, *"Come to me ... and learn of me"* (Matthew 11:29). Paul said, *"But ye have not so learned Christ; if so be that ye have heard him, and have been taught by him"* (Ephesians 4:20-21). In other words, the central source of all spiritual insight and learning is found when we "come to Him" so we can *"be taught by Him"* and in that way we *"learn Christ."* This is not to learn more about Him but to "learn Him ... hear Him ... and be taught by Him." As the text makes clear, this can only be done in direct, one-on-one encounters with Himself through the Holy Spirit. Of course, it is right that we receive teaching at meetings and conferences, and we are now blessed to be able to listen to many great sermons by digital means. However, I fear that we have allowed what is, in effect, a one-step-removed, external form of communicating "truth" to become a substitute for this most amazing privilege of an intimate, direct pupil / teacher encounter with Him who is "The Truth" through the Holy Spirit.

John points us to what should be our central source of revelation and instruction. *"But as for you, the anointing which you received from Him abides permanently in you; so then you have no need that anyone should instruct you. But just as His anointing teaches you concerning everything and is true and is no falsehood, so you must abide in Him [being rooted in Him, knit to Him], just as [His anointing] has taught you [to do]"* (1 John 2:27 AMPC).

It is as we "abide in Him" as described in this verse that the foundational roots of our being go deep into Him. We become "rooted in Him" and "knitted to Him." In this inner place we receive instruction and revelation directly from "The Teacher." Jesus reinforced this truth in John 16:13: *"When He, the Spirit of truth, is come, He will guide you into all truth."* I used to understand this as leading me into a correct doctrinal understanding of biblical truth. No doubt that may be included but this speaks about much, much more. This is the process where we are led *"into all Truth"* so it becomes incarnate and functional in our experience.

For me, the Scriptures began to come alive in a way I had never experienced. The Holy Spirit began to teach me and impress upon me truths which previously I had only understood intellectually. He brought verses to my attention, and I began to see them as never before. What I'm saying is that biblical truth moved from information believed to substance enjoyed!

This is hardly surprising, though, since we are here interacting with the author of the Scriptures Himself. Surely, He is the one best placed to bring us into the enjoyment of that to which they point. Indeed, Jesus Himself said the Scriptures are the signpost which God uses to "testify" or "point us" to the treasures that are ours "in Christ." He said, *"Ye search the scriptures ... and they are they which testify of me"* (John 5:39-40). The signpost is vital of course. It is indispensable, utterly reliable, and our essential plumb line, but it is still a signpost that "testifies" to someone beyond itself. Christ alone is the reality and the destination to which it points!

This process we are discussing is described in the Gospel of John as *"feeding"* directly on Christ. *"For My flesh is true and genuine food, and My blood is true and genuine drink. He who feeds on My flesh and drinks My blood dwells continually in Me, and I in like manner dwell continually in him"* (John 6:55-56 AMPC). Notice that Jesus connects the activity of *"feeding on His flesh and drinking His blood"* directly with abiding or *"dwelling continually in Him."* Just to be clear, feeding on Him is not studying the Scriptures to gain a correct theology, important as that may be. It is waiting and engaging directly with Him. The point I'm making here is, this is not primarily an intellectual activity; it is spirit communing with Spirit! In stillness and in silence we can come to intimately "know" Him. "Inner Knowing" replaces "believing." We worship in spirit and in truth, face to face, all separation now removed as the reality of our union with Christ is experienced in increasing fullness.

This leads us into the experience and reality of Psalm 81:16, *"With honey from the rock I would satisfy you"* and we discover the joy of Psalm 119:103: *"How sweet are your words to my taste, sweeter than honey to my mouth!"* This is the place where we are taught how to drink honey from the Rock and enjoy His beautiful, glorious, satisfying Presence! A child of the Father feeding on and drinking in the honey of His Presence! I think the Passion translation captures this reality so vividly from Psalm 63:5: *"I overflow with praise when I come before You, for the anointing of Your Presence satisfies me like nothing else. You are such a rich banquet of pleasure to my soul."*

This is the worship and intimacy the Father seeks, *"But the hour cometh, and now is, when the true worshippers shall worship the Father in spirit and in truth: for the Father seeketh such to worship him"* (John 4:23). To worship in spirit and truth is to worship in "spirit" reality. This can only happen when our soul, which includes our intellect and reasoning capabilities have been stilled, and the "self-life" is no longer driving our agenda. This is the interaction our Father seeks!

Chapter 18

"Abiding" in Our High Tower

As we "abide in the vine" we begin to realise that we are abiding under His covering and care and that His bounty is flowing freely into our lives! We now find ourselves living in the ecosystem where the rule and reign of the King has jurisdiction, and we discover the promise in Matthew 6:33 that *"all these things shall be added to you"* is now in operation. Righteousness, peace, and joy increasingly becomes our experience. This expands our outlook since our abilities no longer define our possibilities.

That said, I find that satan is most subtle in his attempts to get us out of that "abiding" mode by getting us into seeing our circumstances through the natural lens alone. In the course of our everyday lives, the challenges and difficulties we encounter can cause us to forget we are in union with Christ. What is happening in the natural realm can make us feel like we used to feel: alone, vulnerable, and separated from our divine source. It's a lie of the enemy of course, but if satan can get us back to focusing on ourselves, as if everything is down to us, we very quickly lose our joy and our peace. His objective is to stop us living out of the fullness of our new identity in Christ, and if he succeeds in that, we find ourselves back operating out of our "old self."

We can counteract this if we diligently *"hold the beginning of our confidence stedfast unto the end"*[58] and remind ourselves that we are a

---

58 Hebrews 3:14

"new self." That means affirming that *"we are made partakers of Christ"*[59] and we are *"complete in Him."*[60] If we are "made partakers of Christ," we are partakers of all that He is and all He has accomplished! If we have Him, we are complete with His completeness, fully resourced and totally equipped, for *"His divine power has bestowed on us [absolutely] everything necessary for [a dynamic spiritual] life and godliness, through true and personal knowledge of Him who called us by His own glory and excellence"* (2 Peter 1:3 AMPC). Notice the past tense of the verb there. It is saying that we already have been given everything we will ever need to make it in life and to live a vibrant, Christian experience because Christ in us, living as us, is not just enough, He is exceedingly, abundantly above and beyond what we can ever need, think or imagine!

It's important to recognise that much of the input we receive through our five senses and our natural reasoning can be influenced by ideologies, designs, and strategies of the "god of this world." If we allow him, he uses what we see in the natural to "sabre rattle" and threaten us, creating fear, anxiety and hopelessness. This is just like the waves of the sea as they continue to roll in a never-ending tide of restlessness caused by the wind and storms on the surface.

It is vital, therefore, that we learn to live from "spirit" realities that are continually in play in our "new self" as opposed to the ever-changing fluctuations of our souls. These are the fixed facts of who and what we now are "in Christ." As we do that, we can remain unfazed by all the uncertainties of life because we are rooted in this unseen realm. This is just like the calmer waters deep below the surface of the ocean. What is happening on the surface has little effect.

These spiritual realities can become more real to us than what we detect with our intellect and natural senses. I found that it is as we wait in His Presence, as we talked about in the last chapter, that our

---

59 Hebrews 3:14 AMPC
60 Colossians 2:10

anxious and troubled souls are brought effortlessly back into alignment, and we recover a true perspective of what is reality. "Waiting" is our acknowledgement that we can't fix ourselves or improve ourselves. Our waiting becomes our declaration that He is our "fixer" and our ongoing "keeper."

I know of no other way that we can bring our souls under the direct influence and operation of the Holy Spirit. It is in "waiting" that we recover our equilibrium and get our thinking recalibrated as we settle back into our core centre! Waiting in His presence is where our hearts are strengthened and where the victory is secured. Take a glass of dirty water and let it sit for a while and soon all those dirt particles settle at the bottom of the glass leaving the water clear. Waiting in God's presence, in stillness, has a similar effect. We find all the "stuff" that keeps us so busy, anxious, and hurried begins to settle down, and the Holy Spirit is then able to reignite these spirit realm realities in us.

We see this exemplified in the lives of some Old Covenant characters. They looked beyond what was happening in the natural and saw into this other dimension of reality and lived from that perspective. Many seemed to have a deep, intimate experience of the divine presence which, I suspect, dwarfs much of Christendom's reality today. Isaiah said, *"But they that wait upon the LORD shall renew their strength; they shall mount up with wings as eagles; they shall run, and not be weary; and they shall walk, and not faint"* (Isaiah 40:31). It is wonderful to discover that waiting on God is how our strength can be renewed, how our peace and joy can be restored, and our burdens and fears can be lifted off our shoulders. Some Psalms even use the same "abiding" or "dwelling" terminology which Jesus used. Psalm 91:1, for example, says, *"He who dwells in the secret place of the Most High shall remain stable and fixed under the shadow of the Almighty"* (AMPC). It's evident that for the psalmist this was a profound reality. This was a real encounter which, for him, had real consequences. If we read the remaining 15 verses, we discover the very many blessings which flowed to him as a direct consequence of "dwelling in the secret place of the Most High." These included protection, safety, health, and much more!

The key point we can take from this is that there is a divine source of provision and protection available to those who "abide in the vine" and live in the divine presence.

The following Scripture brings us to the same conclusion: *"One thing have I asked of the Lord, that will I seek, inquire for, and insistently require: that I may dwell in the house of the Lord, in His presence, all the days of my life, to behold and gaze upon the beauty, the sweet attractiveness and the delightful loveliness of the Lord and to meditate, consider, and inquire in His temple"* (Psalm 27:4 AMPC). The psalmist clearly had a strong expectation, unlike many today, that it was possible for him to *"dwell in the house of the Lord, in His presence, all the days of his life."* We are clearly not stretching it too far when we say that the New Covenant, which is based on better promises, can deliver no less than what the psalmist enjoyed under the Old Covenant. Now notice the consequences of *"dwelling in the house of the Lord"* as stated in verses 5-6: *"For in the time of trouble He shall hide me in His pavilion: in the secret of His tabernacle shall He hide me; He shall set me up upon a rock. And now shall mine head be lifted up above mine enemies round about me"* (Psalms 27:5-6). If we do the same, will this not bring us into the same place of protection, where we are *"hidden in His pavilion ... in the secret of His tabernacle, set high upon a rock"*?

This same point is reinforced in Psalm 62. *"For God alone my soul waits in silence: From Him comes my salvation. He alone is my rock and my salvation, My defence and my strong tower; I will not be shaken or disheartened"* (Psalms 62:1-2 AMP). This highlights the thought that God Himself, not a belief system or a doctrine, not attending a certain church, but the immediacy of His very Presence becomes our source from which deliverance and provision comes. This was where the psalmist became aware of his strong tower, where he experienced an impenetrable protection, security, and deliverance.

In fact, Psalm 23 makes it clear that the reason the psalmist could say, *"I will fear no evil"* was precisely because he could say, *"Thou art with me."* It is in dwelling *"in the secret place of the Most High"* that we find ourselves *"stable and fixed under the shadow of the Almighty."* This is *"abiding in the vine"* but described in Old Covenant language.

Jesus, speaking to the nation of Israel, gave us a clear picture of this in Luke. He said, *"How often I have wanted to gather your children together [around Me], just as a hen gathers her young under her wings, but you were not willing!"* (Luke 13:34 AMP). Israel didn't accept this invitation, but even little chicks do this intuitively. This is their birthright. The mother's role is to provide a place of shelter, safety, and rest. The chicks' role is simply to take up a position under her wings. To "abide in Christ" is to do the same as those little chicks, where we run into Christ's Presence for shelter.

We can confidently conclude then that Christ Himself, immediately present in our experience, is our shelter, resource, and deliverance! Salvation is a person; security is a person; deliverance is a person! Psalm 91 confirms that, *"I will say of the Lord, He is my Refuge and my Fortress, my God; on Him I lean and rely, and in Him I [confidently] trust!"* (Psalms 91:1-2 AMPC). Then in verse 4 the psalmist uses the exact same picture as Jesus did in the verse quoted above from Luke 13. He says, *"He will cover you and completely protect you with His pinions, And under His wings you will find refuge; His faithfulness is a shield and a wall."* The place of refuge is found only "under His wings," in other words that place Jesus called "abiding in the vine."

This is the Kingdom operating in our lives where *"all these things are added to us"* (Matthew 6:33) and every need is supplied. Isaiah, talking about God's people in the Old Testament, said, *"And the angel of His Presence saved them: in His love and in His pity He redeemed them; and He bare them, and carried them all the days of old"* (Isaiah 63:9). Psalm 34:7 says something similar. *"The angel of the Lord encampeth round about them that fear Him, and delivereth them."* The terminology "the angel of the Lord" in the Old Testament is seen by scholars as an earthly manifestation of God or the pre-incarnated Christ. *"The angel of His Presence saved them"* ties our deliverance directly to knowing and abiding in His presence. Romans 8 reinforces that same thought: *"If God is for us, who can be against us? Who can be our foe, if God is on our side? He who did not withhold or spare even His own Son but gave Him up for us all, will He not also **with Him** freely and graciously give us all other things?"* (Romans 8:31-32 AMPC—bold mine). Who can be our foe if we have become one with Christ? He is the infinite bringer "of all things" (i.e., salvation, protection, and provision).

Protection and deliverance are not things He gives as something outside of Himself or in addition to Himself, it is He Himself who is all those to us! Therefore, to abide in Him and enjoy His Presence is to abide in His safety, provision, and His infinite supply. Psalm 27:1 makes this very clear: *"The Lord is my light and my salvation; whom shall I fear? The Lord is the strength of my life; of whom shall I be afraid?"* To grasp the truth that *"The Lord is the strength of my life"* is a wonderful, freeing reality. This means our strength is no longer in ourselves and our ability to get everything right but it is in Christ.

As I said earlier, much of this can remain as merely mental information which is of little value. Our hearts are not changed by just mentally holding certain biblical facts. It is as we wait on God, resting in His Presence that the Holy Spirit energises these realities to us, making them vital and real to us on the inside. *"Now we have received ... the spirit which is of God; that we might know the things that are freely given to us of God"* (1 Corinthians 2:12). Indeed, I discovered that it is as we wait in His presence that He energises and connects our faith to these infinite resources and blessings that are already ours in whatever form they may be needed.

I say all of that simply to emphasise this one key elemental understanding. If we have Him as a vital, internal conscious reality, then we already have everything else besides. Paul prayed for the Ephesians: *"The eyes of your understanding being enlightened that ye may know ... what is the exceeding greatness of His power to us-ward who believe ... not only in this world ... "* (Ephesians 1:17-23). This makes it clear that the *"exceeding greatness of His power"* is working for us today in the here and now, not just in the future! The *"eyes of our understanding"* need to be opened, however, so we can grasp these realities in this unseen dimension! This happens when we take time out to wait on Him.

Indeed, if we are "abiding in the vine," living out of our union with Christ as we have been discussing, then our days of defeat and failure have ended and we can start to *"reign in life through the one man, Jesus Christ!"* (Romans 5:17). This means acknowledging that what we see in our natural circumstances are not the final arbiter. They are subject to change as we now have free and welcome recourse to a higher authority! Overcoming can now become our direction of travel and our natural destination. Overcoming is a natural part of the new creation identity. *"For whatever is born of God is victorious over the world; and this is the victory that conquers the world, even our faith"* (1 John 5:3-4 AMPC). Paul puts it this way in Romans 8: *"Yet amid all these things we are more than conquerors and gain a surpassing victory through Him Who loved us"* (Romans 8:37 AMPC). Why is that? Because *"Ye are of God, little children ... because greater is He that is in you, than he that is in the world"* (1 John 4:4).

So we see there is only one reality now for those who "abide in Christ." We no longer "see" our lives from the "natural" perspective. That is, we no longer see our lives through the input we receive from our five senses and our rational minds alone, because we are now "Spirit" realm people. We have access behind the veil that separates these two dimensions of reality. We now abide "in Christ" as our keeper, our shepherd, our impregnable High Tower. All we see is that we are one with Christ who is now living our life. Now *"our lives are hid with Christ in God"* (Colossians 3:3). That is our only point of reference!

At the risk of repeating myself, this must all become "inner knowing"; that is, it must be more than information we read in the Scriptures, it must become real to us and alive in us. This is what happens as we wait on Him by the Holy Spirit. It is there that He fires our vision, our boldness, and our faith! *"Honor and majesty are [found] in His presence; strength and joy are [found] in His sanctuary"* (1 Chronicles 16:27 AMPC).

Paul made this amazing statement: *"For no matter how many promises God has made, they are 'Yes' in Christ. And so through him the 'Amen' is spoken by us to the glory of God"* (2 Corinthians 1:20 NIV). This is saying that every promise of supply, deliverance, and wisdom, and every request will be met with a divine "yes." Since we are "in Christ" the door into the divine storehouse, which is Christ Himself, has already been left wide open to us. We present our requests to the Father as if we were asking on Christ's behalf, on His merits, and in His name, using His credit card if you like! We can go further and say, in effect, as if our requests were being made to the Father by Christ Himself. Would the Father ever deny the Son? I think not! That is an incredible truth to ponder! Isn't this what Jesus said? *"In that day you will not [need to] ask Me about anything. I assure you and most solemnly say to you, whatever you ask the Father in My name [as My representative], He will give you. Until now you have not asked [the Father] for anything in My name; but now ask and keep on asking and you will receive, so that your joy may be full and complete"* (John 16:23-24 AMP).

That is a life-altering truth if we can grasp it. This allows us to operate with a great deal more confidence because we know we have a divine *"Yes"* waiting for us as we *"fearlessly and confidently and boldly draw near to the throne of grace ... and find grace to help in good time for every need [appropriate help and well-timed help, coming just when we need it]"* (Hebrews 4:16 AMPC). This truth puts our needs, concerns, and anxieties into a totally different perspective. Our anxious hearts can be stilled, and the challenges we face in life lose their power over us.

Chapter 19

...Boldly...Obtaining...

The earthly name given to God's Son was "Jesus." It is breathtaking to realise that in the original Greek the name Jesus means "Jehovah is Salvation." That's who and what He is! That is His natural disposition! So, it is inconceivable that, if we are united to Him and we "abide in Him," that is, "abide" in this "Jehovah is Salvation" reality, for that not to usher us into a place where we experience salvation, safety, supply, and deliverance in our everyday lives.

That's not to say we won't experience trouble and difficulty. Jesus Himself said we would experience these but He didn't stop there. John 16 is clear about that: *"I have told you these things, so that in Me you may have [perfect] peace and confidence. In the world you have tribulation and trials and distress and frustration; but be of good cheer [take courage; be confident, certain, undaunted]! For I have overcome the world. [I have deprived it of power to harm you and have conquered it for you.]"* (John 16:33 AMPC). This is our victory: If we wait on Him as we have described, we are ushered into "perfect peace and confidence" that will not disappoint despite whatever difficulties we face. This is how we can be sustained and overcome in all the trials, pressures, and frustrations of living in a fallen, broken world.

Let me give a practical example of what I'm talking about. I had wanted to invest in some property and found a new, light industrial, commercial unit with great offices in a good location, finished to a high specification. I thought I would have no problem renting it and so was optimistic that this was a sound investment. Furthermore, Hazel and I had taken time out to pray and seek God's leading in this as it was a big decision for us. Previous attempts to purchase other premises had proved problematic and, due to unforeseen circumstances, we were prevented from completing. Now, however, we felt we had a green light to proceed. I also felt I was being a good steward over the resources God had given me.

I negotiated what I thought was a fair deal, bought the property, and put it up for rental. Although I secured several short-term tenants, I found the market began to change so that the prospect of securing a long-term tenant was now not so good. After a couple of years of hoping something would turn up, I became quite concerned. In the natural there was nothing more I could do to secure a tenant. However, I knew I had recourse to a higher authority, and I didn't believe that what seemed to be happening in the natural had the final say on any outcome.

Isaiah says, *"For from of old no one has heard nor perceived by the ear, nor has the eye seen a God besides You, Who works and shows Himself active on behalf of him who [earnestly] waits for Him"* (Isaiah 64:4 AMPC). As a result, I began to take time out to simply "wait on God" about this in the way described earlier. I began by unloading the weight of it and rolling the pressure and worry I was holding in my heart over into His hands. This takes time! However, as you unload and unburden your heart, you soon find yourself increasingly being silent since there are only so many times you can present an issue to the Lord without endlessly repeating yourself. This is where faith needs to be engaged and you come to a place where the silence itself becomes an expression of our deeper longing and heartfelt need.

Within a relatively short time, perhaps several weeks, I began to feel confident that God was now at work. I found my concern and frustration began to change to one of optimism, expectation, and hope.

This wasn't me trying to be positive, rather, I believed this was the Lord changing me on the inside to reflect His heart and desire. I don't think I received any promises or verses from Scripture but, nevertheless, I noticed this inner change was taking place.

I also began to realise something very strange was happening at work. Our order intake began to rise dramatically. The market was not particularly good but we began to secure an unusually high number of very high value orders. Soon it became clear we would have to expand the business by taking on more staff and securing larger premises. The shareholders asked me to start looking for suitable property around the Lisburn area as this was close to where we were already and it had good motorway access.

I had decided not to mention anything about my own property even though I thought it would have made a great building for the company. There were two reasons for that. One was that the shareholders wanted a place in Lisburn, and my property was in Antrim. Secondly, and more importantly, I had learnt not to try to engineer my own deliverance by trying to orchestrate something in my own strength. I decided I would say nothing about my property and would continue to wait on God for His supply and deliverance. It had to be Him who did it!

The level of sales in the company continued to grow for no apparent reason. At the time I didn't connect this to the fact that I was being single-minded about "waiting on God." However, by the time we started the following financial year it was clear that we were enjoying a real outpouring of God's blessing and favour. Sales turnover tripled and profitability quadrupled. This was unprecedented! It was rather surreal to see things ramping up like this without any obvious explanation. Since we were not doing anything different to what we had always done I began to realise that something was up and that God was somehow on the move. Nevertheless, all these sales gave a real sense of urgency to finding a larger building with better facilities.

Over a period of time I set up quite a few appointments to inspect various properties in the Lisburn area but none of them seemed to suit our requirements. I was struggling as all the properties available had something about them that made them less than ideal.

One day I received a call from the main shareholder. He told me that he had been in the Antrim area, and he wondered if perhaps this might not be a better location for us. He had been visiting one of our customers there and had noticed some very nice properties which, unbeknownst to him, were in the same area as my unit. He asked me to investigate and to set up visits to potentially suitable premises.

You can imagine how I felt when I took that call! This was "the cloud as small as a man's hand" which Elijah saw. It was then I knew I had my answer. I was filled with an inner assurance that God had heard me and, in His love and goodness, had undertaken to bring about a set of circumstances which answered my need completely.

The following week I arranged several visits to prospective premises but again I didn't mention that one of the properties belonged to me. The visits to the other properties went well but for different reasons they just didn't quite meet the main shareholder's expectations. I left the visit to my own property to last. When he walked in, he looked very pleased and was quite taken with it. He said to me, *"This is ideal, this is the one for us!"* We got back into the car and I now felt I had to tell him that I owned the building. I didn't know how he would respond to that but there was no reason not to tell him now that he had selected the property without any influence or prompting from me. There were several other events which were quite remarkable which showed beyond doubt that this was all God's doing. To cut a long story short, I moved the company into my property about six months later.

As I look back at this, I am overwhelmed by what the Lord did for me. To think that He would bring in such a large harvest of sales to the company in order to create the need for new and larger premises is wonderful. However, to then bring the shareholders to my doorstep without any input from me was just amazing. This was His wonderfully creative way of meeting my need!

I share this story simply to show that with God all things are possible. Not only that but He is willing and eager to come to our rescue as we read in this verse: *"For the eyes of the Lord run to and fro throughout the whole earth to show Himself strong in behalf of those whose hearts are blameless toward Him* (2 Chronicles 16:9 AMPC). As we wait on Him and continue to abide in Him, He is then able to bring about change. He is able to orchestrate circumstances in ways that are so far-reaching and so far beyond anything we could even think or imagine. This is all an aspect of "abiding in Christ" and one which I have found to be a key to unlocking God's supply and provision in many different ways. This is learning to draw everything from Him!

There is a very clear parallel in the Old Testament which underscores this principle. When the nation of Israel walked in obedience to God, fulfilling the precepts and ordinances prescribed by God, relating to worship in the tabernacle or the temple, then the nation as a whole prospered. Their enemies were defeated and there was a tangible increase in the blessing and provision they experienced. Remember, God's desire for them and promise to them was that they might enjoy "a land flowing with milk and honey" which is a picture of abundance and blessing.

However, the reverse was also true. When they went after false gods and stopped honouring the vital presence of God in their midst, their enemies prospered and overcame them. In extreme cases they were even taken captive and completely subdued, becoming slaves to their enemies. Their response to the divine Presence had a direct correlation to whether they lived victorious, fruitful, blessed, carefree lives or a defeated, broken existence. These things were written for our benefit.[61]

---

61 Romans 15:4

Living our lives in union with Christ and knowing His Presence as our centre cannot fail to bring about the same victory, protection, and blessing. Isaiah beautifully describes this life for us: *"And the effect of righteousness will be peace [internal and external], and the result of righteousness will be quietness and confident trust forever. My people shall dwell in a peaceable habitation, in safe dwellings, and in quiet resting-places"* (Isaiah 32:17-18 AMPC).

This was the psalmist's expectation as well when he said, *"Surely or only goodness, mercy, and unfailing love shall follow me all the days of my life, and through the length of my days the house of the Lord [and His Presence] shall be my dwelling place"* (Psalm 23:6 AMPC).

In other words, it is The Transforming Presence of God that enables us to live a life beyond our ability!

CONTACT THE AUTHOR

Email
thetransformingpresence@gmail.com

INSPIRED TO WRITE A BOOK?

Contact
Maurice Wylie Media
Your Inspirational Christian Publisher

Based in Northern Ireland
and distributing around the world.
www.MauriceWylieMedia.com

Lightning Source UK Ltd.
Milton Keynes UK
UKHW022210050922
408362UK00008B/1766